D0381969

Earthlings

Earthlings

IMAGINATIVE ENCOUNTERS WITH THE NATURAL WORLD

Adrian Parr

Columbia University Press
New York

Columbia University Press
Publishers Since 1893
New York   Chichester, West Sussex
cup.columbia.edu

Copyright © 2022 Columbia University Press
All rights reserved

Library of Congress Cataloging-in-Publication Data

Names: Parr, Adrian, author.
Title: Earthlings : imaginative encounters with the natural world / Adrian Parr.
Description: New York : Columbia University Press, 2022. |
Includes bibliographical references and index.
Identifiers: LCCN 2021048071 (print) | LCCN 2021048072 (ebook) |
ISBN 9780231205481 (hardback) | ISBN 9780231205498 (trade paperback) |
ISBN 9780231556026 (ebook)
Subjects: LCSH: Natural history. | Environmentalism. | Nature—Effect of
human beings on. | Biosphere.
Classification: LCC QH81 .P37 2022 (print) | LCC QH81 (ebook) |
DDC 508—dc23/eng/20211104
LC record available at https://lccn.loc.gov/2021048071
LC ebook record available at https://lccn.loc.gov/2021048072

Columbia University Press books are printed on permanent
and durable acid-free paper.

Printed in the United States of America

Cover design: Adrian Parr
Cover images: foxypar4, MaxFaleel, Just Chaos, AMagill,
q.phia, L_, topgold, Image Catalog, wildxplorer.
All images courtesy of Creative Commons.

To Lucien, Shoshana, and Yehuda

Contents

Acknowledgments

I WOULD LIKE TO THANK my colleagues Brad Evans, Jana Braziel, Creston Davis, and Santiago Zabala for their friendship and intellectual generosity.

A very special thank-you goes to my editor at Columbia University Press, Wendy Lochner. I have worked with her for many years and she has transformed philosophy through her sharp, sensitive, and bold editorial acumen.

Morgen Olsen worked tirelessly with me on sourcing the images presented throughout the book. I am immensely grateful for her eye for detail.

I am fortunate to have a spirited and animated constellation of strong, thoughtful, witty, independent women in my life who have provided me with a great deal of unconditional love, support, and encouragement. Thank you. You know who you are.

And finally, Michael Zaretsky, my best friend, partner in life, and my beshert, who from the first day I met him has continued to bring out the best in me.

Earthlings

Commencement

WHETHER WE ARE LOOKING AT the creative life force that science dissects, isolates, documents, and demonstrates; the wonderful and miraculous that myth and literature illuminate; or the transitory relay of life, death, and decay that philosophy ponders and property law captures, it is in the endlessly rich return of the living and nonliving, of abundance and emptiness, and in the undoing of reason and selfishness, that planet earth's disobedience occurs. The earth's defiant insubordination in the face of human will, pontification, and domination has confounded, surprised, and inspired amateurs, practitioners, and the proficient alike; it is indifferent to what you or I think, feel, conjecture, or calculate. Yet despite the autonomy of the earth as a self-regulating living system, one group of organisms has managed to dramatically transform this wondrous and enchanting living system in just a little over two hundred years—a relatively short blip of time in the earth's 4.5 billion–year history. The culprit earthling in question? Humans.

The combined activities of many humans stretched across different generations, nations, and creeds have combined to form a singular material force that has come to shape all manner of life on earth. Since the industrial revolution, the pooled efforts of human labor, leadership, ingenuity, and misguided resourcefulness have consolidated into what many call "global capitalism," "finance capitalism," or "neoliberalism." Without entering into a laborious examination of definitional nuances, the nomenclature simply highlights the manner in which the global economic system that human beings have collectively created, and the subsequent weakening of democratic politics and social inequities that this system has produced, is changing the natural cycles of the earth and placing its entire life support system under stress.[1] When we speak of humans fundamentally changing and compromising earth's life-giving system, we are referring to the ways in which this collective and cumulative human economic, social, and political system works to capture earth's primal growth and reproductive systems and redirect them into an unyielding structure of violence and precariousness waged against trillions of unnamed, unspecified, and unheard beings.

Whether we are speaking of the ongoing slashing and burning of the world's forests; demolition of marine ecologies; erasure of animal habitats; smothering of the earth's organic surface with concrete, chemicals, and trash; pumping greenhouse gases and a horde of other pollutants into the sky; or radically altering the climate system, *Homo sapiens*, the species to which all humans belong, are basically running riot throughout the world's oceans, wilderness zones, ecosystems, and atmosphere. At the rate we are going, the complexity of life on earth will be severely diminished. In the absence of radically changing how human communities live and the priorities used to direct the organization of human societies the world over, which mediate our relationship with other-than-human species, human beings will be responsible for eventually creating an earth that is no longer conducive to sustaining a vast majority of current life on earth—including that of humans themselves. Under these circumstances, the existential question defining the twenty-first century is not *whether* life on earth will persist but rather in what *form* it will it exist.

That said, no matter how much human beings change all manner of life on earth, it is inaccurate to emphasize anthropocentric forces of change over ecocentric ones. Indeed, it would be an anthropocentric exaggeration to underestimate earth's autonomy in this way. The earth is like a single living organism; its life force is spurred on by the interaction of living and nonliving elements that collectively optimize and sustain the conditions for a complex and enriching abundance of life. This life system is unique to the earth, and it persists regardless of how much *Homo sapiens* alter the way it functions. Life on earth will continue, and even recuperate, in spite of the ecological damage humans have and continue to inflict upon it. Humanity, however, through complete fault of its own, may no longer exist to delight in the bounce back.

It is up to us, as a species, to individually and mutually invoke our ethical sensibilities and to extend our imaginative capacities to rediscover our common place alongside the many species, organisms, cells, and molecules that make up the biomes in which we collectively survive and thrive. This is a call to activate transpeciesist, transgenerational, and transnational thinking, understanding, and practices. A call to a transenvironmentalist undertaking that recognizes and supports the mutual imbrication of the earth's life-giving systems in human production, policies, politics, and values. It is nothing short of an invitation to resuscitate our humanity and reinvent how we put it to work.[2]

Scouting out other worlds within the routine of familiarity not only swells the senses but also affectionately unveils the deoxyribonucleic acid (DNA) we share with all manner of life, from the plants populating the surface of the planet to the birds and bees taking to the skies in the breeze. The many threads, lineages, and traces that tie you to me, us to the millions of microscopic life forms making up over half of the human body, through to the underwater invertebrates that share the same evolutionary tree as us, are the many filaments vivaciously forming complex layers of extinction, diversification, evolution, and regeneration, spawning common ancestries and distant cousins traveling back millions of years in time and propelling these forward for hopefully millions more. The breaks, bonds, attachments, additions, and extensions moving from the nanometer to the micro and macro scales make up the rhizomatic threads of life engaging living and nonliving alike. They constitute the many materialities, forces, energies, and chemical reactions of earthly activity that together generate a kaleidoscopic array of earthlings.

In this book, "earthling" denotes biotic systems metabolizing, moving, growing, reproducing, generating waste, and responding to stimulation, as well as the many interactions they have with abiotic solids, liquids, and gases. Put simply, it is the nonbinary principle of *sharing* common to the thriving vitality of earthling-being that provides our point of departure into a transenvironmentalist journey across time, through the air, into oceanic waves, to ultimately submerge our "selves" in encounters with other-than-human endeavors. Transenvironmentalism is a process of implication whereby the hierarchical organization of human/nonhuman is unraveled to awaken an ecocentrically situated understanding of life that makes us "part of that nature we seek to understand," as Karen Barad has so poignantly stated.[3] It also invokes myriad effects that are harnessed to migrate across and through different bodies and generational perspectives, destabilizing the artificial property lines of nation states and the many economic and social boundaries human beings have established and wielded along the way.

Earthlings share functions. They share characteristics and genetic material. They share ancestry extending back 4 billion years to the last universal common ancestor of all cells, a single-celled bacterium that has gone on to proliferate into the many earthlings that today constitute the complexity and variation endemic to earthling lives.[4] Regardless of whether you support a two- or three-domain model for life on earth, the eukaryotes, archaea, and bacteria making up all manner of life do not coexist independently of each other; they share a context: planet earth.[5] It is amidst this state of sharing that a community of earthlings appears.

Earthlings *share* a planet, and not any old planet. They share a water-saturated planet, the only planet in the solar system that is home to trillions of living beings. It is this singular capacity, or drive, of earthling sharing that lays the foundations for the flourishing for all life on earth. *Homo sapiens* are just one group of earthlings amongst trillions of others.

We humans share histories, ecological networks, and potentialities with an entire gamut of living entities and systems. And together this mishmash of earthly existence is both remarkable and irrelevant, for the earth and universe are indifferent to earthling action, migration, alteration, agitation, or termination. The distinction between the living and lifeless is not one that changes the order of the universe or the movement of the earth. The earth will rotate on its axis each day, orbiting the sun in an elliptical pattern every 365 days, spiraling slightly away from the sun with each year that passes, regardless of whether or not humans populate the planet. Human beings are not the center of the world's forests, oceans, prairies, mountains, rivers, lakes, and skies. The earth is not the center of the solar system, nor is the planetary system in which the earth and seven other planets orbit the sun the center of the Milky Way galaxy. The Milky Way, in turn, is just one galaxy amidst billions of others in the universe.

Thinking and imagining across scales in space and time situates us and our earthling neighbors in a much larger context. The journey can be expansive and hypnotic, even as it is sometimes unsettling. *Earthlings* takes us on a vicarious and sacred voyage through the unfamiliarity latent in familiarity, bringing us up close with those hostile and beautiful moments composing life on earth. Consisting of a series of portraits, the stories at the center of *Earthlings* explore and play with the sensorial range and affective reach of plants, vertebrates, and invertebrates as these interact with landforms, settlements, climatic conditions, and oceanic systems. Alternating between fiction, myth, science, anthropology, and philosophical reflection, *Earthlings* is testament to how the innumerable and nameless lives making up the trillion other-than-human species on earth illuminate and magnify our humanity. The labyrinthine machinations of viruses, flora, fauna, animalia, wind, waves, and organismic genetic material mingle and connect in weird and wonderful ways. Ultimately, *Earthlings* is a saga about providence, prosperity, tenacity, exceptionalism, and injury.

Art and literature invite us to come alive. Medicine and science try to keep us alive. The law tells us how to live. Politics questions how we live. Religion hopes to give us something to live for. Philosophy pursues how living and nothingness work, tempting us to explore what we love most about life. This book is a little of all of these, and hopefully something more.

{ 1 }

Land

ITS TWO-HUNDRED-FOOT-LONG BODY bent in the breeze, offering itself up to the moist fog and darkened skies. A cone loosely attached to one of its dry, awl-shaped leaves fell quite suddenly, surprising the mule doe and her fawn below. The fallen cone released its frost-tolerant seedlings into the earth, eager for sunlight to return. Members of the group, fellow great sequoias (*Sequoiadendron giganteum*) located two miles away, briefly hesitated, then rocked back and forth with the wind as it declared itself. Birds and lodgepole chipmunks anxiously scratched their way around the tree's brittle limbs, seeking refuge from the storm. The slow breath and soft body heat of a spotted owl, snuggled inside its trunk, warmed the gaping hollow near its base. Underneath, the sequoia's roots stretched out across the land, its xylem tissues soaking up minerals and water, transporting these throughout its parched woody tissue, up into its foliage.

The rain brought welcome relief from a prolonged period of drought. The dense forest vegetation had been thirsty for years. When the snowpack higher up the mountain decreased, the rushing streams transporting nutrients slowed to a trickle as their average water temperature rose. The cold-blooded salmonids, which flourish in cooler conditions, had become stressed. They moved constantly from one part of the stream to another, desperately trying to thermally regulate their bodies. When the cold-water refuges disappeared, stream flows changed and higher water temperatures normalized. Fish started to lose the temperature cues that enabled them to locate food and avoid predators. At a higher, more remote location of the forest, another fish, not native to the mountain lakes, was wreaking havoc on the mountain yellow-legged frog population, greedily consuming tadpoles. The tadpole-eating trout combined with a new frog-killing fungus and with pesticides blowing in from the valleys below, decimating this once thriving amphibian population. Here in the wild, the wind and water benefit some and are a burden for others.

The rains had failed to come, year after year. What little water remained in the tree's leaves had evaporated. Then, after the soil moisture declined, photosynthetic activity dwindled. Under these arid conditions, the tree's growth was stunted. Overwhelmed by water stress, its body no longer reproduced. The previously collaborative root systems of the forest, now exhausted, had begun turning on each other. Where previously the trees had cared for and supported weaker members of the community through a vast underground social network, they now, in thirsty desperation, robbed one another of vital water resources.

Bark beetle infestation broke out amongst the vulnerable, voraciously boring into their living tissue and feeding off of their phloem. The warmer-than-usual winter weather meant more beetles survived through to the spring. The beetles laid nests inside the bark, infecting the trees with a fungus that quietly prevented the remaining nutrients from feeding on it. Having discovered a patch of weak trees, the beetles released a chemical, known as aggregation pheromones, into the air, alerting fellow beetles of the food source. When they were fully grown and their hunger had been satisfied, the beetles exited, leaving the trees to slowly starve. Tree mortality would later present a fire risk.

The tree sensed a throbbing loss, an echo pulsating deep down throughout its collective root system. It was one of the luckier ones; it had mustered up enough water reserves to produce a resin that could submerge and kill the beetles in its sticky red substance. It became one of the rare ones to survive extreme heat, water scarcity, infestation, and more. Its not-so-hardy friends had long ago perished. Yet the resin-infused bark was both a blessing and a curse, for in addition to fighting off the predatory beetle, its flammability would fuel wildfires.

The heat had taken its toll on forest life. Ground moisture was overdrawn. The lush green canopy turned brown from chronic thirst. When water evaporated from the leaves, trees were forced to draw down even farther in search of water, draining moisture from the soil at a faster rate than the rains could replenish it. Millions and millions of these stoic sequoias died off when the deep soil water vanished and insect contagion befell them. A loss of this magnitude had taken its toll on the once flourishing arboreal ecosystem. Many tree ancestors perished, some more than 3,000 years old.

All was not lost, however. A forest with dead wood blanketing the ground reduces erosion. Dead wood can collapse into streams and become an important source of thermal cover for aquatic life. Fallen logs eventually provide new habitats for woodpeckers, snakes, moss, fungi, lichen, and nesting ducks.

A colony of carpenter ants invaded the damp, decaying wood, using their powerful jaws to chew their way through the log. Working together, they carved out a labyrinthine series of tunnels, leaving a trail of sawdust in their wake. These half-inch-long insects feed on nectars secreted from the glands of other plants, and on a sugary honeydew that aphids emit as the ants stroke them with their elbowed antennae. In the summer months, a hungry omnivorous grizzly and her cubs avidly sniffed the air, tracing the smell of ant pheromones to the nest. The bears ripped the wood apart with their teeth and claws, reaching into the nest with their sticky tongues to feed off of the fat and protein in the larvae and pupae. They left largely untouched the adult ants, who upon being attacked had quickly released a defensive concoction of citronella and formic acid. The bears had started eating more carpenter ants than usual as other food sources in the forest diminished. Over time, the supply of nuts and plants the bears typically feast upon fell, after a water mold pathogen called *Phytophthora ramorum* caused some of the oak trees to die off and blister rust went on to kill many of the sugar pines.

This community of biotic and abiotic earthlings—trees, leaves, bushes, grasses, mammals, birds, amphibians, fishes, arthropods, reptiles, microorganisms, water, wind, sunlight, and more—are different but related. In the forest, the well-being of one is clearly implicated in the flourishing of another. Climatic fluctuations and extensive social ecosystems made up of roots, hydrologic flows, and biological legacies connect earthlings across manifold spaces and times. The ecological value of this community far surpasses any kind of measurable economic value people may attempt to place on it. The intriguing and limitless cycles of ingenuity, sustenance, and death, through the mixing of chemical compounds, gases, energy, matter, bodies, excretions, and flows, make up the productive and reproductive forces driving all life on earth. James Lovelock called this super self-regulating organism Gaia.[1]

The fundamental lesson of Gaia is that earth is a system out of which no living being can feasibly extract itself, a fact too eagerly and often dismissed by zealous reasoning and technological hubris. Gaia flies directly in the face of human exceptionalism. We humans do not inhabit the earth as discrete entities. Life, and by extension the earth, does not succumb to human will. Indeed, humans are the effect of a complex system of temporal and material enfolding: big bang atoms of hydrogen; stardust atoms of carbon; nitrogen and oxygen; then genes that have traveled across time to blend with molecules, cells, chemical elements, and gases, which are structured into organs, bones, hair, nails, and skin as well as nervous, lymphatic, and renal systems. All these elements clash and connect to form an atonal musical of sorts, regulating body temperature, expelling waste, and moving oxygen around.

It would be remiss to assume that Gaia exists in a state of harmony. Our bodies, like the terrain on which we live and the biospheres in which we are implicated, are riddled with struggling bacteria, mites, fungi, viruses, and protozoa battling out their existence. Our bodies provide a rich habitat for a multitude of parasitic microbiota living on and in our bodies. More than 99% of the octillions of atoms making up our bodies are in fact largely empty.

Greek mythology also acknowledges that life originated out of an abyss of sheer emptiness. In *Theogony*, Hesiod tells of the emergence of the earth goddess (Gaia), the underworld (Tartarus), and love (Eros) from the infinite depths of vacuity. Gaia produces the sky (Uranus) and together they create the Titans, the one-eyed violent giants (Cyclopes), and the hundred-handed giants (Hekatonkheires). Disturbed by their massive size and repulsive appearance, Uranus imprisons the Cyclopes and Hekatonkheires in the belly of the earth, causing Gaia terrible suffering and pain, a pain so acute that she convinces her son, Kronos (time), to kill his father. Upon castrating Uranus, Kronos casts his father's testicles into the ocean, and then, as the blood of Uranus mixes with the sea, Aphrodite, the goddess of beauty, love, and sexuality, comes into being.

According to legend, the headstrong Kronos becomes the ruler of the heavens, oceans, and earth, yet he remains haunted by his father's curse, that his own child would one day kill him. In an effort to negate the prophecy, Kronos devours his children at birth—until one day his wife, Rhea, saves their youngest child, Zeus, the god of the sky, thunder, lightning, and justice. Zeus kills his father, forcing Kronos on his deathbed to cough up Zeus's siblings and bring them back to life. Filled with a desire for vengeance, Zeus wages war on the Titans and wins.[2] He becomes the prime ruler of the gods and mortals, controlling the world with brutal force, serving as both judge and peacemaker.

Hesiod's creation story paints a picture of life that is as much a regulatory mechanism maximizing habitability as it is violently disruptive. The life-sustaining figure of Gaia, representative of Lovelock's hypothesis, obscures the Darwinian view of violent natural selection, casting aside some of the most self-destructive forces of the natural world, which paleontologist Peter Ward has employed as the basis of a very different kind of creation story. Using another mythological figure from ancient Greece as his point of departure, Ward puts forward an alternative view to Gaia. His Medea hypothesis is one of a biocidal earth. He presents a polemical view of life as having a predatory drive, and his counter narrative of life on earth begins with the sorceress Medea.[3]

Brokenhearted Medea punishes her husband, Jason, for forsaking her for another woman. In an unbridled act of heated revenge, she callously ends the lives of their innocent children. Medea is a spellbinding story of anger unchecked, of ferocious jealousy, and of the deliberate murder of one's own offspring. Medea is thus the antithesis of the archetypical figure of Gaia, who nurtures and sustains life.

Lovelock and Ward are admittedly unlikely bedfellows. However, by combining their divergent perspectives here, I suggest that life is expressed not only in participatory, self-reinforcing patterns of behavior, as Lovelock describes, but also in the specific suicidal and destructive tendencies that Ward outlines. Life on earth is filled with contradiction. It is fragile and ferocious, reticent and tenacious, innocuous and lethal. In sum, the living world is both Gaia and Medea.

The making and remaking of communities—no matter how great or small, simple or complex, structured or unstructured they may be—all pivots, by and large, around assembling something in common. This includes the way in which the earth soaks up water and minerals and then the manifold ways in which root systems distribute themselves throughout the earth and transport nutrients to quench the thirst of plants, trees, bushes, and grasses. It is seen in the intimate interaction of breathing foliage, which draws water and minerals from the soil and brings in carbon dioxide from the air, forming a concoction that the warm rays of the sun energizes, transforming carbon dioxide (CO_2) and water (H_2O) molecules into rich combinations of glucose and oxygen. These, in turn, are released back into the air, ready for other animals, like us human beings, to use to replenish our bodies.

Photosynthesis is a collective interaction of gases, molecules, chemicals, and energy. It forms a community that generates the basis of ecological flourishing. That is, until divergent earthlings, driven more by individual gain than by collective well-being, thrust the system into turmoil, making it dysfunctional. Gaia is filled with bad actors who are poised not simply to disrupt but even to demolish Gaia.

Just think of our own species. There are 7.8 billion people living on the earth, and we are projected to reach 10.9 billion by the end of this century.[4] The carrying capacity of the earth—the number of people the earth can feed, clothe, house, warm, cool, and transport—sits between 9 billion and 10 billion people.[5] Once we start consuming the earth at a faster rate than it can replenish, we exceed the earth's carrying capacity and we kill the very source of our own flourishing.

To understand the contradictory makeup of living systems and their distinctive life forms, human beings offer up some important lessons. People are terrestrial animals, yet we are cavalier and brutal in our treatment of the very land on which we depend for our survival. We stick dynamite into the peak crevices of mountains, gashing into the planet with bulldozers and drills. In the past, worker humans with headlamps and picks were sent deep down into the hot, dark depths of the earth to extract coal, oil, metals, minerals, and aggregate. Today, in the United States, coal mining is a much simpler undertaking: entire mountains throughout the coal country of Appalachia are amputated. The distinctively green, leafy, undulating topography of the region has been replaced with maimed earthly bodies artificially restructured into a series of dark gray parallel flats.

In U.S. coal country, humans have restructured the geography and chemistry of the earth—and the bodies of the miners as well. They suffer from higher rates of birth defects and mortality than nonmining Appalachian communities and live in a lethal mixture of geographic isolation, drug addiction, poverty, and a failing educational system.[6] The nationally subsidized coal industry and the corporate coal moguls running the Appalachian mining enterprise have stripped the mining communities of their unions, a decent living wage, and their health.[7]

This is one case amongst countless others where both land and people are sacrificed for the elixir of economic excess. We burn fossil fuels to warm our bodies in the freezing cold and to cool ourselves when the summer heat becomes overwhelming. Coal, petroleum, and gas feed the energy grid powering our domiciles, skyscrapers, transportation, and manufacturing. The machinery used to fertilize, irrigate, grow, process, package, and refrigerate the meat, vegetables, fruits, cereals, milk products, eggs, and nuts we eat all rely on pumping gases such as carbon dioxide and methane into the atmosphere, each and every second, 365 days a year, year in and year out. In 2007, food production in the United States alone was responsible for 13.6% of all global fossil fuel CO_2 emissions. Put differently, that amounted to 817 million of the approximately 6 billion metric tons of CO_2 emissions that year.[8]

The approximately 57.3 million square miles of land on the earth is nearly 30% forest,[9] but this is being cleared by human beings at a rate of a little more than 50,000 square miles per year. This is one of the main drivers of global climate change and land warming.[10] The World Resources Institute reports that from 2015 to 2017, tropical tree loss resulted in an average of 4.8 gigatons of carbon dioxide being released into the atmosphere each year.[11]

Those magnificent carbon sinks, the earth's forests, absorb around 30% of heat-trapping carbon humans spew into the atmosphere.[12] However, Medea is giving Gaia a good run for her money: humans are producing heat-trapping gases faster than the world's forests can absorb them, and humans are consuming the world's resources at a ravenous pace, much faster than the earth can restock them—and many of these resources cannot be renewed. The forests of the Global South, which are more effective than their northern forest compatriots at trapping carbon, are now being belligerently removed, in both the literal and the metaphorical senses of the term *belligerent*.[13]

On March 31, 2020, the bullet-riddled body of the Amazonian forest protector Zezico Guajajara was found dumped on the dirt access road leading to his village, Zutiwa.[14] The murdered Brazilian director of the Indigenous School Education Center of Azuru was the fifth Indigenous rights leader within a five-month period to have been killed trying to stop the illegal logging of the Amazon's Arariboia rainforest. From August 2018 to August 2019, Amazonian deforestation increased 222%.[15] The Guajajara people draw physical and spiritual sustenance from the Amazonian land. But then Brazil's president, Jair Bolsonaro (elected October 2018), took the cultural value Indigenous groups ascribe to the forest and wielded it as a weapon against them. Justifying the recent uptick in the removal of Amazonian forest since entering office, Bolsonaro maintained that the slashing and burning of the world's largest and more ecologically rich rainforest was merely cultural.

We have seen this before, thought Olimpio Santos Guajajara, head of the Guardians of the Forest.

First, it was the Indigenous rubber tapper Chico Mendes, who had fought to save the forest and, because of it, was assassinated in his backyard by cattle ranchers in December 1988. His death famously threw the plight of Amazonian deforestation into international consciousness. The plight of the Amazon was part of a long, messy, and bloody history of land theft, intimidation, violent coercion, fear, and murder. The Brazilian military dictatorship from 1964 to 1985 had trampled all over Indigenous rights, killing Indigenous peoples and dispossessing them of their lands to make way for highways, dams, and mines. These people were then forced to work for the very enterprises that had destroyed their way of life. When the military regime fell, Indigenous groups were allowed to petition for the return of their historic lands. Brazilian president Fernando Henrique Cardosa (1995–2003) ratified 118 Indigenous land applications. His successor, Luiz Inácio Lula da Silva (2003–2010), approved eighty-one new Indigenous reserves, but the enthusiasm he and Cardosa had shown for Indigenous and environmental rights quickly dimmed when President Dilma Rousseff (2011–2016) took over the country; she approved a mere eleven Indigenous reserves.[16]

The *grileiros* (illegal land grabbers) moved quickly, burning the undergrowth, carving out trails, and dividing the land into lots ready for agricultural production. The fifty-foot *Coccoloba* tree with its eight-foot-long leaves stood quietly witnessing the violence erupting along the edges of the Uru-Eu-Wau-Wau Indigenous territory. The reserve is 6,950 square miles and it sits in the West Brazilian state of Rondônia. This great *C. gigantifolia* tree, as the scientists call this species of *Coccoloba*, was one of the fortunate ones, as only 30% of its Amazonian companions outside the borders of the reserve remained.[17] *Grileiros* regularly invade the forest armed with rifles, threatening the Indigenous peoples who stand in their way. The *Coccoloba* is reminded of the village elder Bitete Uru-Eu-Wau-Wau, who received death threats for protecting the land, and his friend Uaka, who complained to the National Indian Foundation (FUNAI), but then no law enforcement arrived to stop the illegal loggers. The *grileiros* had filled Uaka's small but strong body with bullets, adding two more just for the fun of it, a threatening reminder to the villagers, should they dare to report them to the authorities again in the future.

The Señor, as they call him, is chief of this rainforest's mafia. He can undermine the dignity of even the most brazen member of the Jupaú tribe with threats and a cockeyed smile. Upon inspecting Uaka's still body, he seized Uaka's headdress of parrot feathers and the collar of otter teeth adorning his neck; this was the Señor's trophy kill, and the Señor made sure he had souvenirs to prove it. The blue-black *jenipapo*-painted shape, reminiscent of open wings, spread across his chest, a symbol of war, had begun to fade. Uaka had been one of the brave ones, a *Jururei*, as his grieving family and friends called him. The arrows he used, made of parrot and eagle feathers, were no match for the ammunition and the unsentimental forest thieves using it against him. The 2.7 million Indigenous groups comprising 350 ethnic groups living in the Amazon biome are the primary custodians of the earth's lungs and protectors of 10% of the world's biodiversity.[18]

One year elapsed, and another grave misfortune overcame the *Coccoloba* tree. Lumbermen audaciously arrived in the dark of night, working swiftly so as not to alert the locals in the nearby Jupaú village. They cut a tree ten feet away and dragged its still-living body through the forest, trampling saplings and the thick biomass lining the forest floor, which had been fertilized by phosphorus-rich dust blown from the African continent.[19]

Weeks later, another group of humans arrived, this time in the hundreds. They were a mob of cattle ranchers, and the barrels of gasoline they dragged with them betrayed their pernicious intent. Clearly deficient of any moral compass or respect for the law, they set the ancient forest alight. On the verge of asphyxiation from the thick gray smoke, and absolutely helpless, the *Coccoloba* tree stared down in despair at the three hundred or so Jupaú villagers who were forced to flee. The fires were so vast, people reported, that the smoke could be viewed from space. If outsider diseases such as flu and measles didn't kill the Jupaú, then the theft of their birthplace, the land stolen right from underneath them, would. Cheated of their livelihood, and their protective forest spirits now all dead, they abandoned their *malocas* (longhouses) and hammocks. The military planes circled above, dropping water to squelch the inferno, but to no avail. Then came the bulldozers, hauling the trees from the forest with chains. The biomass and stumps presented a challenge for ranchers eager to turn the land over to industrial agriculture, so they torched the remains. The forest lay in ruins.

Mortified by the insanity of it all, the *Coccoloba*, once a light-hearted species, turned from the sun's rays. Heavy with sadness, the tree's leaves drooped toward the thick vegetation below. It was shattered to have been orphaned this way. Now, not even the village elders could save the forest from commercial exploitation. The forest would help the carnivorous humans gratify their hungry desires with burgers, hot dogs, and steak, to fill their tanks with biofuels, and to consume many other agricultural commodities, such as soy and sugarcane, that the once richly biodiverse land could help provide. As the tree canopy shrank, so too did the forest's capacity to generate rain.

The far-right Brazilian president, Bolsonaro, had unleashed a new era of Amazonian destruction. The question for the great *Coccoloba* was how would arboreal animal populations, the millions of insects, the thousands of bird species of the forest, and the world's climate endure this next chapter in the Amazon's long 55 million–year history?[20]

Three hundred and ninety billion trees, made up of 16,000 different tree species, together cover the 2.1 million square miles of the Amazon, crossing nine national borders throughout South America.[21] Commonly referred to as the "lungs of the earth," the Amazon breathes in carbon and releases gigantic amounts of oxygen into the atmosphere. A mere 1% of the total tree species in the Amazon are responsible for 50% of the forest's total carbon sink.[22] However, these numbers fail to capture the full injury and shock that a landscape besieged with unmarked stumps and animal remains emits.

If humans continue at the current pace of unbridled deforestation, the forests of today will be ghostly remnants of themselves by the end of this century. How we live on the land, the changes we make to it as forests are slashed, burned, and cleared, are problems we all share in common with other-than-human species and with the Indigenous tribes trying to fend off loggers and ranchers. Each year, 24 billion tons of fertile soil are lost because of land degradation.[23] Deforestation, overgrazing, the loss of topsoil, and erosion and nutrient depletion are leading to ever-increasing losses in soil function and to land warming. Over the past six decades, the average temperature of the earth's land has warmed 2.3°F. This is twice the rate of global climate warming.[24]

As the surface of the earth burns up, land moisture levels drop even more, turning once lush landscapes into harsh, arid environments, making the injured land more susceptible to desertification.

How we tend the land and care for it directly impacts the ability of the earth's soils to sustain human and other life forms. As the world's land is mined, built, and industrialized, the fertility of the soil is compromised, but without fertile soil, stable food production systems across the world cannot be maintained. Degraded terrestrial ecosystems affect the vitality of watersheds and biodiversity health, yet we humans return time and time again to pick over old wounds, regardless of how crippled and maimed the land is, stripping it of all it's worth, until there will be nothing left to share. It is the ultimate betrayal.

And the land cried out, "How much is enough?"

{ 2 }

Parasite

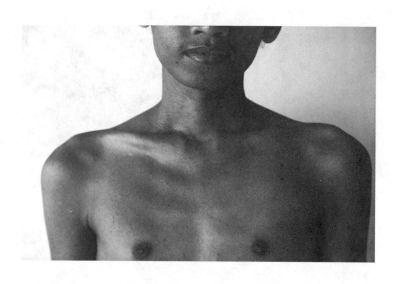

THE MOSQUITO PERCHED at a 45-degree angle on the side of a sweat droplet, her black and white scaled wings hovering in the optimal temperature of 80°F.[1] She let her tentacles wander over the pores of his sprawling body, closely studying the movement of skin in sleep. His bright blood, all sweet and tempting, enticed her needle-long mouth (proboscis) to navigate the grassland wilderness of body hair and crevices in the search of a perfect feeding site. If it weren't for the flexibility of her proboscis, the blood-meal mission would be severely thwarted. Her probing lasted a mere second or so. Settling her belly down, she opened her legs wide, all six of them, resolutely positioning herself, ready to sink her mouth in.

With a clear, decisive bite, she pierced a capillary, quickly and methodically injecting a stream of anticoagulant saliva into the wound to avert the blood from clotting. This allowed her enough time to feed without her elongated mouth getting stuck there in the drying liquid. Her saliva set off an allergic reaction in the host and the site began to swell from an infusion of histamine. Time was of the essence for this hungry mosquito, as the defensive release of the chemical had alerted the nerves encircling the bite site. It would be a matter of seconds before Jorge would feel an intense urge to itch.

Consumed by an insatiable maternal instinct to access the nutrients offered by Jorge's human blood, and by a desire to produce the eggs she needed to reproduce, the *Anopheles darlingi* rushed to finish feasting. Full to the brim, the blood-engorged insect was ready to return to the swamp. She brushed past Jorge's ear, buzzing with contentment. The meal had taken her no more than ten seconds to complete, just enough time for the *Plasmodium vivax* that had grown in her gut to be released into another host: an overworked and exhausted body, deep in slumber at the edge of dawn.

The *Anopheles darlingi* had ingested the malaria parasite while pumping infected blood from the sawmill manager, Joao, just eight days before. The parasite had been dormant in Joao's liver for months. However, upon entering the body of the *Anopheles darlingi*, the parasite mated in her gut (gametocyte stage). After quickly replicating, it traveled to her saliva glands (sporozoite stage), where it then passed into the sleeping Jorge.[2] In its new host, the malaria sporozoites rapidly moved to his liver (becoming hypnozoites), where they asexually multiplied, developing into active schizonts, which in turn produced more parasites (merozoites) that were able to leave Jorge's liver and surge throughout his blood stream.[3] In Jorge, the single-celled *Plasmodium vivax* parasite could burrow its way into his red blood cells because it attached to Jorge's Duffy glycoprotein, an important chemical receptor that enabled the *P. vivax* annexation to occur. Had his blood been Duffy-negative, as is true of many people in West Africa, transmission would have failed.[4]

This is how malaria invaded Jorge, a thirty-two-year-old immigrant worker. He had moved to the Amazonian logging settlement of Boa Vista do Pacarana just months ago. Desperate to provide for his family, he decided to try his financial luck as a timber harvester. His plan: work ten months logging in the Brazilian municipality of Espigão d'Oeste, then return home for two months. Having been laid off from his job at the citrus processing plant in São José do Rio Preto, he had searched six months, in vain, for another minimum wage position. It was then that he made the difficult decision to trek approximately 1,300 miles across the country to earn a living for his wife, Aurea, and their three children, Antonio, Carlos, and Gardenia.

Neither he nor Aurea had graduated elementary school. Although Aurea worked part time cleaning homes, her meager earnings were not enough to cover their monthly expenses. It was not long before they slipped from poverty to extreme poverty, moving from a small house with running water and electricity to one without. Illiterate, unskilled, and determined that his three children would graduate secondary school, Jorge left the neighborhood he grew up in for an ten-foot-high cement block structure at the edge of the Brazilian Amazon forest.

He labored hard, he labored long, sawing and hauling heavy hardwood logs. Worn out before each day began, his fatigue came as no surprise. Had it not been for the harsh working conditions, he would have taken the time, spent the money, and seen a doctor. Instead, Jorge was fooled into thinking all he needed was a little more rest. Then came the crippling nausea and continual puking, leaving his mouth sour from heaving bile. Nights later, he awoke to a burning sensation that brought lightning flashes to his eyes; his head was thumping to the earsplitting beat of raindrops on tin. Defeated by chills that rattled his skeletal frame and caused the soft tissues connecting his bones to ache all the more, Jorge mistakenly dismissed these symptoms as stomach flu.

The parasite held steady. The bedridden host was now shivering in a lively febrile sweat, hovering on the brink of impenetrable blankness. Within days he stopped urinating and his body swelled. He billowed in and out of consciousness. He thought he could hear the sounds of Gardenia and Carlos laughing, of Antonio kicking a ball with impatience, and his beloved Aurea whispered his name from the light-filled edges of darkness. Time slowed. Outside, the hustle and bustle of ambition and anticipation looked down on an uncharted life now unexpectedly quiet. It was seven in the morning on February 3, 2018, that Jorge Pereira died of acute tubular necrosis.[5] He was about to turn thirty-three years old; instead, tears streamed down Aurea's inconsolable cheeks.

Malaria is endemic to the Amazon, with approximately 99% of all cases reported in Brazil occurring there.[6] The increasing incidence of malaria, though, is linked to anthropogenic land use changes. In their research on malaria transmission rates in deforested areas of the Amazon, Andy MacDonald and Erin Mordecai concluded that it is both an environmental and a human health issue. Comparing malaria and deforestation data, they found that increases in deforestation correlated with more incidences of malaria. Interestingly, the more that malaria presented in a given area, the more deforestation decreased. It is now widely known that deforestation rates of the Amazon rainforest have spiked since Brazil's President Bolsonaro took office in 2019. From January to April 2020, 464 square miles of the world's largest forest was cleared because of illegal logging and mining. This marked a 55% increase over the same period the previous year. However, an increase in Amazon deforestation is not only an environmental issue that results in biodiversity loss and the shrinking of one of the world's most important carbon sinks; it also impacts public health.[7]

Comparing geospatial data sets for 795 Amazonian municipalities over a thirteen-year period (2003–2015), MacDonald and Mordecai found a strong correlation between rates of deforestation and malaria transmission. More specifically, their research shows that a 10% intensification of Amazon land clearing can be connected to a 3.3% increase in the incidence of malaria in the area. To put it in concrete terms, that amounts to 9,980 additional cases for 2008. The reason why is that deforestation creates forest edge zones, the prime breeding habitat for the *Anopheles darlingi* vector. Forest edges are positive larval habitats for the *Anopheles darlingi* because changes in forest cover produce variations in shading, hydrologic cycles, and vegetation. Settlers also create artificial bodies of water, such as ponds and wells, which provide additional habitats conducive to larval development. Roads and ditches offer spaces for ground pools to form after heavy rains.[8] As people migrate to high-malaria mosquito zones, the human-to-mosquito contact rate grows, and along with this, biting incidences rise.

A rather unexpected effect of increased malaria in forest-edge Amazonian communities is that it generates a biodirectional socioeconomic feedback effect. In addition to increased malaria rates in deforested areas, MacDonald and Mordecai also found the increase in malaria incidence decreased the rate of deforestation. They estimated a 1% increase in malaria cases produced a

1.4% decrease in deforestation.[9] This was a surprising outcome of their research on land use and vector-borne pathogens, and it casts a spotlight on the nonlinear and interdependent modalities of exchange occurring amongst molecules, cells, tissues, organs, bodies, ecological elements, and behaviors. Unearthing the mutual imbrication of public health and ecology in this way prompts us to reconsider major public health challenges beyond the frame of individual treatment and diagnosis.

In response to a malaria epidemic in the 1940s that was infecting approximately 6 million people each year, the Brazilian Ministry of Health, in collaboration with the World Health Organization, turned its efforts during the 1950s toward disease eradication. By taking measures such as spraying inside walls with DDT and treating febrile individuals with chloroquine, Brazil managed to lower the annual number of malaria cases across the country to 36,900 cases by the 1960s. However, as a wave of new settlements and gold mining activities started to take place in the Amazonian regions from the mid-1960s onward, a new influx of malaria cases occurred. As many as 578,000 were reported in 1989.[10]

The Brazilian government responded by shifting its focus away from disease eradication and onto treating and diagnosing individual cases. Although the number of treatment and diagnosis stations across the Amazon grew substantially, leading to a decrease in disease severity, over time it was not enough to slow malaria transmission. A wicked problem had surfaced at the interstices of four different trends: climate change, deforestation, escalating migration to the Amazon, and treatment resistance.

Now we return to the biodirectional feedback loop MacDonald and Mordecai describe. By environmentalizing the social field as much as socializing ecology, their findings encourage us to think about health beyond the frame of *public* health and to pay closer attention to modalities of disease distribution by taking into account the sociality immanent to ecologies, and ecologies as immanent to the social. Disease dynamics are synergistically complex and noncyclical; they are neither unidirectional nor reliably predictable.[11] Disease distribution dynamics are complex and move using nonlinear modes of interaction. Rather than deploying reductionist models that focus on identifying a sequential series of relationships $(1 + 1 = 2)$, more recent health care studies and practices incorporate systems thinking and modeling into diagnosis and treatment.[12]

Often, minor and sometimes seemingly unrelated disturbances in an ecological–social–epidemiological system can create major impacts, such as significantly higher incidences of malaria emerging out of deforestation practices, whereby deforestation rates actively respond to an increase in malaria cases by dropping. This ebb and flow of real circumstances and their extant materialities coincide, and together they realize variables and variations immanent to their respective conditions at a specific place and moment in time. Put simply, disease exists in the flow of time. Consequently, disease needs to be broached with the understanding that earthlings are not a reflection or a causal effect of a given ecological circumstance, nor do the material realities of earthlings (such as disease) and their associated activities instantiate ecological conditions. Rather, the situation of one is an emergent quality of the other. The change in logic is from a mimetic understanding of the real (that is, it reflects an underlying form) to a creative and productive understanding of reality (or continually forming and reforming existing elements and their aggregation).[13]

The complex machinations of diseases endemic to specific geographic areas, the destabilizing effects of epidemics on local populations, and the disastrous consequences when epidemics transform into pandemics that occur at a global scale present an opportunity to consider the many -demics (endemic, epidemic, pandemic) in question from the vantage point of open situatedness. The notion of "open situatedness," in the way that I am using it here, refers to operationally unstable interactive configurations, the boundaries of which are energetic and leaky. They have three organizational characteristics: transnational, transgenerational, and transpeciesist.

The human immunodeficiency virus (HIV) epidemic is a revealing example of open situatedness. It emerged through the mixing, scattering, and coalescence of a multiplicity of formative agents—human and other-than-human biology, urbanization, and changes in land use patterns, poverty, sexuality, and health care. Since the HIV epidemic began in the early 1980s, more than 32 million people have died of the virus and 75 million people have been infected by it.[14] Scientists have struggled to find a clear point of origin for the virus, although they believe the first recorded case of HIV-1 viral infection occurred in 1959 in Kinshasa (known at the time as Leopoldville), in today's Democratic Republic of Congo. However, HIV-1 sequence data evidence shows infection was regional as early as the 1920s in Kinshasa.[15]

A combination of social and environmental factors led to the spread of HIV. Until the 1950s, the disease moved throughout the DRC along trade routes, before eventually spreading throughout sub-Saharan Africa. By the 1960s, Kinshasa was rapidly urbanizing. New trade routes in the area opened up as transportation infrastructure expanded, allowing people to move across greater distances at a faster pace. A gender imbalance set in, as many more male workers and traders entered the area, facilitating a thriving sex economy. Loose health care practices further increased infection rates.

The two types of immunodeficiency virus that develop into acquired immunodeficiency syndrome (AIDS) in humans, HIV-1 and HIV-2, emerged when a particular strain of the simian immunodeficiency virus (SIV) jumped from nonhuman primates to people.[16] In Africa, SIVs are endemic to monkeys and apes. Over time, the viruses moved many times across different monkey and ape species. Throughout this transgenerational and transpecies process of SIV movement, novel combinations and mutations of the virus occurred until a strain emerged with the capacity to jump to humans: SIVcpz. More specifically, SIVcpz materialized when the SIV strain in red-capped mangabeys combined with another strain of SIV from the greater spot-nosed monkey, with *Pan troglodytes troglodytes* chimp populations in southern Cameroon serving as the host.[17] Humans acquired the virus from monkey and chimpanzee bushmeat. Inside a human, the SIVcpz modified into the deadlier version of HIV (HIV-1). With each jumping event—monkey to chimpanzee to human to human—the SIV adapted and changed, until eventually many different HIV-1 strains came into existence in humans. Meanwhile, the less infectious HIV-2 virus developed from the SIVsmm strain found in sooty mangabey monkeys.[18]

HIV infection in people arose from a series of multilayered temporalities involving incremental changes through mutation, evolving over time and across geographic locations, as well as from radical moments of change with each cross-species transmission event. Analysis of the HIV-1 genetic history shows that the virus circulated amongst human bodies throughout the Congo for several decades at the beginning of the twentieth century, prior to spreading to other countries across Africa. Infection rates sped up under Belgian colonial rule of the Congo, when new temporal layers arose from an expanded transportation infrastructure, and then the transmission pace picked up again as the disease entered the hustle and bustle of city life on the African continent. After the virus traveled to the Americas, infection rates took on another tempo, moving rapidly in the spaces of air travel and bathhouses, via sexual contact, blood exchange, and needle injection.[19]

The HIV epidemic can also be described as having an inside-out organizational structure. It replicates with the use of a host and then self-replicates once it is inside a human T cell. Because the virus needs to occupy a host to replicate, it has a sympoietic life cycle that requires externalities to grow. At the same time, the HIV epidemic can be described as autopoietic, for once the virus attaches to the human T cell of white blood cells, the virus replicates itself inside the cell and then discharges the additional HIV into the blood, where the process of replication begins all over again. This is why antiretroviral drugs work best in a person who is in the early stages of the disease.

The inside-out organization of HIV is further shaped by asymmetrical geopolitical power relations situated at the interstices of church and state, by the global free market in big pharma, by social and economic inequities that have resulted in women being disproportionately impacted by HIV, by homophobic stereotypes that perpetuate HIV vulnerabilities in gay and bisexual communities, and by the stigmatization of substance abusers as unable to adhere to HIV/AIDS treatment, limiting the scope and availability of treatment programs for them.[20]

Last but not least, as a complex series of -demics, HIV has a transversal spatial character. It destabilizes and scatters across borders demarcating nation states, bodies, species, geographies, and genetic types. It forms a smooth spatial organization—in blood, breast milk, and semen—that allows for easier transfer into a new host. Once inside a host, it distributes itself rhizomatically, undergoing multiple moments of division, discharge, and dissemination both within a given body and as a bodily excess that transfers into another body.

HIV forms an infected body by attacking its immune system and slowly destroying its T cells. Having no universal structure, it mutates as it disseminates, with broad geographic dispersion. It moved from the African continent to Haiti in the mid-1960s—though some maintain it moved from the United States to Haiti with sex tourism.[21] Regardless of the exact migration route, by the mid-1980s it was on five continents (Africa, Australia, Europe, North America, and South America).[22] The historical lineage of the virus also brings to light an assemblage made up of different scales of instantiation, from genetic diversification (HIV-1 has mutated into nine subtypes), to being endemic to individual species (certain species of monkeys and chimpanzees), to infection at the scale of an epidemic (in the Congo, and later in Haiti and the United States), until eventually it grew to the scale of a pandemic with international reach.[23] As a zoonotic disease, HIV renders borders porous and supple, rupturing the fixed relations that constitute territories, such as individual species, bodies, and even genetic types.[24]

Nearly 60% of human diseases are zoonotic. David Quammen writes, "Bubonic plague is a zoonosis. All strains of influenza are zoonoses. So are monkeypox, bovine tuberculosis, Lyme disease, Marburg, rabies, Hantavirus Pulmonary Syndrome, and a strange affliction called Nipah, which has killed pigs and pig farmers in Malaysia, as well as people who drink date palm sap (sometimes contaminated with the virus from bat droppings) in Bangladesh. Each of them reflects the action of a pathogen that can cross into people from other species."[25]

Zoonosis refers to bacterial, viral, or parasitic diseases that can spill over from vertebrate animals to humans.[26] Examples of zoonotic diseases include bubonic plague, Ebola, avian flu, severe acute respiratory syndrome (SARS), HIV, and more recently, the coronavirus SARS-CoV-2, which can lead to COVID-19. Zoonotic viruses are endemic to certain species that, despite the virus living in them, remain asymptomatic. Ascertaining which animal serves as a reservoir host for a zoonotic disease is an important first step in stopping further outbreaks, slowing the rate of infection, and eventually creating a vaccine.

In addition to identifying a patient zero as the basis for zoonotic disease diagnosis and treatment, more attention needs to be paid to how spillover works. Zoonotic transfer occurs when people venture into the habitats of wild animals to hunt or to remove trees, as human settlements grow along forest edges and human beings and/or their domestic animals come into closer contact with wild animals, or as wild animals lose their habitats to deforestation and are forced to venture closer to human settlements.

In December 2013, an eighteen-month-old boy from the small, remote village of Meliandou, Guinea, which includes only thirty-one households, used a hole in the base of a tree to play hide-and-seek. Here, he came into direct contact with infected bat poop. Two days later he was dead. He became known as "patient zero" for the deadly Ebola virus disease that spread at a vicious pace throughout West Africa. The World Health Organization's Public Health Emergency of International Concern status, placed on West Africa because of the Ebola outbreak, wasn't lifted until March 29, 2016. The Ebola outbreak had lasted two years, killing 11,325 people, mainly in Guinea, Liberia, and Sierra Leone. A total of 28,652 cases of Ebola had been reported in that time.[27]

Meliandou is located in the forest region of Guinea. Linking ecological changes in the area to the Ebola outbreak, the World Health Organization explained that much of the surrounding forest area has "been destroyed by foreign mining and timber operations. Some evidence suggests that the resulting forest loss, estimated at more than 80%, brought potentially infected wild animals, and the bat species thought to be the virus's natural reservoir, into closer contact with human settlements."[28]

The escalating global practice of removing old growth forests to open up land for human development is bringing people into closer contact with wild animals, and along with it, the transmission of zoonotic infection is growing. Recent studies on the transmission of zoonotic infection connect the increased levels of infection to anthropogenic land conversion.[29] Mining, agriculture, and urbanization all are changing the landscape through the removal of trees, and animal habitats are fast disappearing. The growth of human activities in, around, and between forests influences human behavior, providing more instances for nonhuman animal source host and recipient host species to contact humans. The thinning and eventual loss of thick forest cores, as well as a growing number of human communities living along forest edges and in between forest patches, are creating conditions ripe for zoonotic parasites to jump into human populations.

Six-year-old Changying edged cautiously toward the side of her grandfather's disheveled bed. When her *yeye*, as she called him, had gone off to the hospital, her throat had ached for days from the sadness trapped there. Changying dropped her legs to the side of the empty bed; they were barely long enough to reach the saffron-colored carpet. She dingle-dangled her limbs there for a few moments until the tip of her toes discovered her yeye's neatly placed fur-lined winter slippers below. The slippers had sat in exactly the same spot, waiting for her grandfather Kong to return.

Changying slipped her bare feet inside the slippers, feeling the imprint of her yeye's feet against hers. She sat there, twisting her cold toes against the cozy lining, waiting for them to warm her skin. As she abruptly straightened her knees, the left slipper flipped from her foot. She shuffled across the room to collect it. The bedroom still carried the faint odor of her yeye's cinnamon-scented hairstyling wax. She went to the window, her tiny feet dragging the oversize slippers across the floor. Each night, she quietly waited here, watching the street, eager for him to return home. The windows were sealed shut, protecting the room from the freezing river winds outside. Kong never appeared.

Kong is a classic Chinese name that means "sky." He was raised by a peasant family in the heart of rural China. As a teenager, he had worked the earth with his father during the week. Weekends were spent courting Ai amidst the sound of running water along the luscious banks of the Gan River, far away from the quick tongues of idle village gossip. In the ensuing years, they lost the farm to a developer, who replaced the rice fields with a large factory that spewed smoke no matter whether it was day or night. Kong found work at a local wildlife farm. The breeder raised many varieties of *ye wei* (game meat) for city traders: king cobras, rattlesnakes, rat snakes, civet cats, even peacocks.

When his boss began hiring members of his own family to work the farm, Kong received fewer and fewer shifts, so he supplemented his meager earnings by raising bamboo rats. He kept the rodents in stacked cages in the courtyard he shared with his three neighbors. He continued in this way until the time came to leave the rural village where his ancestors had lived for generations, to try his luck in the city. He, Ai, and their ten-year-old son, Liang, traveled by train to Wuhan, a city in the next province. His skills in the *ye wei* industry earned him a job working at an outdoor stall in the western zone of Huanan Seafood Market. He spent the workweek slaughtering and preparing meat for sale, and it was here were he caught the wretched disease in a split-second spillover event. Some believed it came from pangolins; others claimed bats. On January 1, 2020, the market was suddenly closed in an effort to contain the outbreak.[30] Eleven days later, Kong fell ill.

The forty-nine-year-old Kong rode his bicycle to Wuchang Hospital to receive treatment for what seemed to be symptoms of pneumonia: fever, diarrhea, vomiting, muscle aches, and chest pain. The next day he lay still, inside a whiter-than-white room, on a bed as stiff as a chopstick, sedated, with a tube down his throat, surrounded by medical staff in white protective suits. A loud regular-sounding machine drove high-pressure oxygen into the air sacs of his failing lungs.

Drifting in and out of consciousness, Kong remembered the first time he and his wife met. She had accidently tripped and dropped her rucksack in the mud on the way to school. Kong had stopped to help her clean it off. They were classmates at the local village school in Jiangxi province. She would wear her thick, straight black hair neatly divided down the middle and then formed into two shoulder-length braids, which she adorned with brightly colored silk ribbons. But the memory faded there and Kong slipped back to darkness. Hours later, his body glided around the edges of awareness, summoning forth the warmth and happiness he had felt with the birth of their son, Liang. He remembered the brightness that had filled his heart when he first glanced upon his baby boy. And then he sank into the hollow darkness again. The treatment at Wuchang Hospital failed to stop the virus robbing his lungs of breath. Eventually, his exhausted body could no longer cope. The emergency alarm sounded. Kong was unplugged at 2:43 P.M. on January 28, 2020. Cause of death: severe acute respiratory syndrome coronavirus 2, or COVID-19.

The knot in Changying's throat broke free and sorrow consumed her thin physique. The smog-filled skies of the city were clearing. She looked out the window at the clouds passing by, a Chinese symbol for luck. She watched the frosty winds whirl across the steel gray sky outside. She thought she spotted Kong amusing himself in the place where dragons were said to play and fly. For a fleeting moment, she caught a glimpse of her yeye stretched out in the yin and yang of air and water. Her eyes followed the blooming lines of changing cloud formations, never tiring of the motion. But thinking about it more, she realized it was Kong vanishing into the heavenly skies forever.

{ 3 }

Migrations

A PANDEMONIUM OF FELLOW MIGRANT MONARCHS (*Danaus plexippus*) from central and eastern North America pirouetted through her legs, brushing against her body and nuzzling into her head. She was swaying and twirling in and out of the sun's rays, relieved to have arrived at her wintering grounds in the Transverse Neovolcanic Belt of Mexico. Weeks earlier, the circadian clocks in her antennae had prompted her to leave southern Canada and head in the direction of the equator. She had flown thousands of miles, guided by her internal light-sensitive magnetic compass and the position of the sun. She had ridden the waves of warm air currents on sunny days, tumbling into and along deflective wind currents passing over buildings, bridges, and barricades, until she eventually floated and fluttered her way into the cloud coverings of the Michoacán forest.[1] Here, migrant monarchs abounded, infusing the thick, moist, dark green environment with hues of rich velvet orange. They would spend four to five months wintering together in silence.

Snuggling into a cluster of 15,000 other monarchs covering the bough of an eighty-year-old oyamel fir (*Abies religiosa*), she closed her wings and hung there motionless amidst the pine needles. She had entered a state of hormonally controlled dormancy. The cool temperatures of the forest would slow her metabolism. As long as the weather conditions didn't become too wet, which would make her vulnerable to freezing, and the cloud cover remained intact, which stopped much-needed heat from being discharged (radiational cooling), she would do just fine here for the next few months.

She had never visited the forest before. She had never traveled to Mexico before. She had never made the demanding journey from North America before. As such, this sleeping monarch was oblivious to the fact that this year the forest was filled with half the number of wintering monarchs compared to previous years, 53% fewer to be exact.[2] She was unaware that she would need to draw on her precious lipid resources more than her ancestors had, as the combined surface temperatures of the trees would be 1.2°C cooler than in previous years.[3] She never noticed that the forest had lost around 1,700 acres to avocado orchards to meet the U.S. appetite for green gold, or the fiery geopolitical climate this created.[4] And she had slept silently as a monarch butterfly activist, Gómez González, and a monarch tour guide, Raúl Hernández Romero, from the El Rosario Monarch Butterfly Biosphere Reserve, were discovered dead, believed murdered for resisting the illegal logging industry.[5]

When she awoke 154 days later, groups of monarchs who had clustered along the trunks of the oyamel firs had perished during the unusually wet weather.[6] Now entering a period of sexual maturation, she flirted and cavorted with the equally excited male monarchs. Together they made their way north into Texas, where they would mate and breed. This would be their final stop before dying. In Texas, however, the native milkweed (*Asclepiadaceae*) needed to raise a baby monarch was in short supply. Glyphosate chemicals in weed killer had killed off large patches of the plant, and that, along with increased habitat fragmentation, made it difficult for the monarchs to successfully reproduce.[7]

Having never visited the area before, she was less focused on the dwindling milkweed numbers and more attentive to finding a mate and to sucking on the syrupy nectar juices of flower-filled fields. Unexpectedly, the fleeting fragrance of sweet aromatic milkweed blossoms captured her attention. In an effort to woo her, a male monarch had released an abundance of scented pheromones into the air from the two sacs at the base of his wings. He was now zealously pursuing her, midair. Surprised, she hastily curled her white-spotted black body around, faintly lowering her heavily veined orange wings before succumbing to the weight and force of her mate. Entwined this way, they gracefully dropped from the air. They turned their backs on each other and he dexterously clasped onto her rear end using the organs at the base of his abdomen. They remained connected for more than an hour as he transferred a spermatophore packet from his body into hers.

It contained more than 10% of his body weight and was filled with sperm and nutrients.[8]

Now fertilized, she laid her eggs one by one on the leaves of a milkweed plant, her mate closely by her side. Four days later, in mid-March, a first-generation baby monarch caterpillar came into the world. It and subsequent generations would live up to six weeks, until the super-generation monarchs were born, farther north, in August.

The super-generation monarch caterpillar had been vigorously eating and shitting, day in and day out. Crunching, gnawing, munching, and chewing the bitter-tasting greenish-gray foliage of a wild milkweed plant in the middle of a meadow at the edge of the southern Canadian border. Unlike its first-, second-, third-, and fourth-generation ancestors, who only lived two to six weeks, it would live a little over eight months. It had come into being inside a single butterfly egg laid on a milkweed leaf in late July. It had been unusually hot as the larva germinated inside the hard egg-shell. The wax lining of the shell kept the egg from dehydrating before the animal hatched from it, four days later.

When the miniature caterpillar entered the world, it quickly set about consuming its shell before turning to the abundant foliage of the milkweed plant. As it grew, its milky body color changed to a series of regularly spaced white-, black-, and yellow-striped sections. Its thorax and abdomen rhythmically opened and compressed as it methodically ingested the firm fuzzy velvet leaves. Oxygen entered the animal's body through minuscule holes (spiracles) in its cuticle, spreading throughout its body via a complex system of tubes. Although it had six pairs of eyes, these could really only sense shifts in light intensity, not enough to formulate a clear image of its surroundings. Using its antennae and the hairs covering its body, it navigated its way around the host plant. The hooks on its five pairs of black prolegs tightly gripped the leaf. Its powerful jaws (mandibles) worked hard at cutting off bits of foliage, then its thoracic legs clutched the food and carefully guided it toward the maxillary palps that inserted the meal into the caterpillar's mouth.

This little larva was hard at work filling its body with cardiac glycosides, contained in a white sap that for many animals is toxic but for this tiny creature would provide an important shield against hungry birds and other potential predators. A leaf a day fueled rapid growth, causing its exoskeleton to tighten. A hormonal release of ecdysone enabled it to molt, bringing much-needed relief to the animal as it was now graced with more room to grow. It would have a total of five instar events (the time between skin shedding) over approximately two weeks before it would be plump enough to begin the next phase of its life.

When it reached two inches long, it scouted out a new spot under a twig in preparation for pupation. Here, it hung upside down spinning a silk cushion that attached to the twig. A small, elongated piece of stretched skin (the cremaster) connected its abdomen to the silk button. The caterpillar split open its exoskeleton, shedding it one last time. Now a milky jade green covering (chrysalis) submerged its body. The creature dangled there for eight days as its enzymes (caspases) liquefied the cells in its organs, muscles, and tissue. Through this process of liquefaction, its breathing apparatus remained intact. From here, its previously inactive imaginal discs came to life, each disc multiplying its cells by the thousands in order to create the different parts that would go on to make up an adult monarch.

First, a digestive system was formed, and then, in just a little over two weeks, limbs, organs, and tissues followed, until eventually a monarch butterfly appeared from the fluid mess. It slowly pulsated and pumped its wings, inflating them to the breaking point, cracking open the chrysalis bit by bit with the motion. It eagerly broke free of the transparent chrysalis, spewing out reddish, watery leftovers, the residue of its transformation. Weighing less than a gram and perched on the broken remains of the clear chrysalis, it waited for its crumpled wings to smooth before testing them out. They spanned three and a half inches.[9]

It was 6:40 in the morning and the sun had begun to rise on a cool September day in Ontario. The newly formed super-generation female monarch butterfly began her cross-continent migration. She followed a pollination corridor through the Northeast states of the United States, along the Atlantic Coast to Florida and the Gulf Coast. Food was hard to find as her primary sources of nectar—cowpen daisies, late-flowering bonesets, goldenrods, frostweeds, and Brazilian sky flowers—had diminished over the years.[10] The nectar would be converted into lipids that would provide her with an important source of energy over the winter months.[11]

Crossing the U.S.–Mexico border, the super generation monarch passed through Ciudad Hidalgo, a town in the northeastern Mexican state of Michoacán. The town was filled with candles, bottles of beer and water, photographs of deceased relatives, incense, fruits, sweets, and the signature artifact: a brightly decorated sugar skull (*calaveras de azucar*). Marigold flowers representing the sun abounded; their sweet aroma was believed to help lure the spirits. These were the offerings (*ofrenda*) locals had laid out at altars lining the streets, some of which reached fifteen feet high. The offerings would entice the dead to return. First, departed children would revisit the living, on October 31. Adult spirits would follow, and by November 2 the festivities would reach their peak on Noche de Muertos.

Women filled the public squares, dressed in long, lavish floral dresses, high-heeled black boots, and bloomy headpieces. Men paraded the streets in black tails, white shirts, and black hats adorned with colorful feather displays. Their ghostly faces were painted as La Catrina skulls: black and white, symbolic of death, and accents of red, symbolic of the love felt for a deceased family member. Some even dressed as a brilliant orange monarch butterfly; others had monarchs painted on their festival dresses. Women adorned their thick, dark hair with monarch butterfly hair clips. The annual Dia de los Muertos (Day of the Dead) activities were in full swing, and this little creature was believed to be the soul of the dead revisiting the living. It flew around an altar blanketed with wildflowers and green apples.

There, a small boy excitedly tried to stroke its wings. He gently whispered, "Mariposa monarca; mi tio amoroso, es que tu?" (Monarch butterfly; my loving uncle, is that you?) His uncle, Irepani Ruiz, had died the previous year in the Port Isabel Detention Center in Los Fresnos, Texas. He was twenty-five years old.[12] Mesmerized by the butterfly perched on the altar to his uncle, the child was convinced this friendly little earthling was Irepani's spirit come to visit.

Honest to God, how could it not be! he thought, as he watched the creature move lightly through the air. His uncle had overflowed with kindness and promises never broken.

"A family savior, who always awakened the best life on earth could create," his *mamita*, Guadalupe, said, staring motionless out the window.

"A devoted and passionate husband," Irepani's *esposa*, Bonita, whimpered, heartbroken.

He had been a father, who softly and slowly stroked his daughter Adonia's hair with grace and gentleness, reassuring the anxious four-year-old that he would return again in a year or two, maybe next time for good. An uncle, whose talents with a soccer ball were indisputably priceless. An activist, who advocated for his Ciudad Hidalgo community and migrants' rights, even from afar.[13] His very being . . . healing for everyone, without even trying. Needless to say, Bonita never moved on.

Irepani began courting Bonita Martinez in April 2010. He first caught sight of her selling homemade goods during the festivities of Semana Santa (Holy Week). She had shared her homemade tropical fruit preserves with him. He complimented her on her cooking. Chatting and being friendly to a local girl like this out in public was not scandalous, but it was enough for tongues to start wagging, and even for some to rush to a few shady conclusions. Bonita had the reputation of a good girl: pious, quietly spoken, unassertive, and restrained. Irepani was known for his candor and generosity. He was hardworking, practical, and somewhat hot-headed, but resolutely loyal. So when Bonita's father heard the rumors he sat upright, swallowed hard, lit a cigarette, and gave the situation some thought. His daughter's honor was at stake, and it was up to him, her father, to safeguard it. Irepani and Bonita must marry, he concluded.

It is custom for Indigenous Purepecha couples to marry early. She was fourteen at the time; her groom, sixteen. By early December, just before the Fiesta de la Inmaculada Concepción (Feast of the Immaculate Conception), the couple celebrated an informal union. She was one of 6.8 million girls in Mexico who marry before eighteen years of age.[14] One year later, Miguel was born, marking the time for Irepani to escape poverty and deport himself to join the many undocumented Ciudad Hidalgo migrants sending remittances home.[15]

Irepani moved his wife and newborn son in with his mother and fourteen-year-old brother, Torres, then made his way north. He crossed the border for the first time in November 2011. There, he joined a small Purepecha community living in a mobile home park located on Torres Martinez Cahuilla tribal land. Back in the 1990s, the county had shut down the illegal trailer parks where the Purepechas and other migrant farmworkers lived. Their solution? Move to land outside the enforcement zones of the county code. They lugged their trailers onto Torres Martinez Desert Cahuilla tribal land, paying rent to tribal council member Harvey Duro Sr. Irepani paid $31.25 for an overcrowded and broken-down dark green trailer that he shared with fifteen other people, in a rough-and-ready forty-acre settlement consisting of approximately three hundred trailers housing around 4,000 people. Duroville, with its makeshift electrical wiring, dirty water faucets, broken sewerage lines, dirt grounds filled with feral dogs, and toxic air from the dump next door, was now home.[16]

Initially, Irepani found a few odd jobs to get by. When the high season for agricultural work kicked off, a contractor effortlessly placed him with work in the Coachella Valley citrus fields. The job? Handpicking citrus fruits, day in and day out, no matter what the weather. He earned $10.60 an hour for climbing up and down an aluminum ladder forty-five hours a week, carrying up to eighty pounds of produce, for approximately thirty-six weeks of the year. He would cover his body from head to toe to protect himself from the pesticides and heat exposure. Starting with a bandanna tied around his head and held in place by a baseball cap, followed by jeans and boots he had picked up at a local thrift store, a long-sleeve T-shirt, and then to top it all off, a pair of heavy-duty gloves that extended up his forearms. He worked this way, without unemployment insurance, workers compensation, or health insurance, in up to 120°F heat, sometimes nearly dropping from dehydration because the fifteen-minute walk to the water station required more effort than working thirsty. When he slipped from the ladder and twisted his ankle, he used the migrant health clinic and paid for the X-rays out of his savings. For the sixteen weeks he was not employed on the farm, he worked odd jobs again to make ends meet.[17]

Crop work was impossibly grueling, hot, and unsafe, but it earned Irepani and his family back home $17,500 a year.[18] He had returned home twice—first in 2014, and then again in 2015, for the birth of his daughter, Adonia, and to collect his lofty nineteen-year-old brother Torres and bring him back to California to work alongside him in the fields. After the first week of crop picking, a dispirited Torres collapsed into bed, his dreams drained and his energy exhausted. Together, he and his brother earned $38,000 that year. It was enough to start building a small house on the outskirts of Ciudad Hidalgo. And this was how a concrete, tangible aspiration replaced Torres's ambitions of becoming an artist. The young man was filled with hope again. Some might say it was false hope, but it was hope nonetheless.

Irepani's fateful trip occurred on April 20, when he was captured by the U.S. Border Patrol and fell critically ill while in custody. The authorities gave no explanation; they just announced Irepani had died. Needless to say, when Irepani died, the family looked to his grieving brother for help. Despite the loss Torres felt and the painful urge to return to the familiarity of hometown life in a valley surrounded by mountains, he held his head high, wiped back his tears, and stepped up to the plate. The border had mercilessly swept his undocumented brother's footprints from the earth, and now he was the sole provider for his wife, two children, sister-in-law, nephew, niece, and their aging parents.

As the primary country of destination for global migration, the United States hosts 19% of all global migrants.[19] Calculating the migration flows across the U.S.–Mexico border is difficult, for obvious reasons. There just isn't any way to officially track unauthorized migrants who move back and forth between the two countries. To date, estimates have been calculated using U.S. and Mexican national census data. That data shows that in 2017 there were 11.6 million Mexican migrants residing in the United States, 43% of whom were unauthorized. In 2017, the United States deported undocumented Mexican migrants 192,334 times.[20] After President Donald Trump entered office in 2016, there was an uptick both in implementing harsher immigration policies along the U.S. southern border zone and in inflammatory political rhetoric used by the U.S. administration, describing migrants as a security threat. The militarization of migration is further exemplified by the designation of U.S. Customs and Border Protection (CBP) as a security agency. In a memo dated January 31, 2020, the agency's acting commissioner, Mark Morgan, announced, "I am pleased to announce CBP has been designated as a Security Agency under Office of Personnel Management's official Data

Release Policy, effective immediately. Previously, only frontline law enforcement, investigative, or intelligence positions held this designation. This policy change now protects all CBP employee names from subsequent responses to Freedom of Information Act requests or other public disclosures for CBP employee data."[21]

The new security classification for U.S. Customs and Border Protection adds a whole new level of secrecy to the agency, and it obstructs the transparency of the organization's operations amidst an international and national outcry against cruel and inhumane policies, including separating parents from their children, and the subsequent detention of minors, including toddlers and infants. U.S. immigration authorities apprehended 52% more unaccompanied migrant minors in 2019 than in 2018, detaining a total of 76,020 children.[22] By May 2019, over a twelve-month period, seven children had died while in the custody of U.S. immigration authorities.[23]

A large number of migrants living illegally in the United States are children, and by the end of 2019, approximately 649,000 immigrants who had migrated to the United States without permission as children could now legally work and were protected from deportation under the U.S. Deferred Action for Childhood Arrivals program, or DACA. The largest number of "dreamers," as immigrants protected under DACA are known, came from Mexico (521,440).[24]

As of 2019, nearly 3.5% of the world's human population were international migrants. This amounts to approximately 272 million people who no longer reside in their country of birth, the majority of whom are women and 14% of whom are under the age of twenty years old.[25] The sociopolitical context in which migration takes place dramatically intensified in the early years of the twenty-first century.

There are five prevailing variables that serve as drivers for global migration, and these by no means operate in isolation from one another. The first is conflict: wars in Afghanistan, the Central

African Republic, the Democratic Republic of the Congo, Iraq, South Sudan, Syria, Yemen, and elsewhere have resulted in mass displacements of people, leading to more internal and international migrations. The second factor is economic, an estimated 181 million labor migrants fleeing economic hardship, seeking greater financial stability in other countries, typically in the Global North or the Middle East.[26]

The third migration variable is slavery, and this intersects with both conflict and globalized labor. There is a burgeoning global migration trade in human beings for sexual exploitation or the production of pornographic material, forced marriage, armed combat or other kinds of forced labor, forced criminality, and forced begging. The majority of human trafficking victims are women and girls.[27] The fourth migration variable, genocidal violence, clearly overlaps with social conflict. For instance, the massacre and persecution of the Rohingya Muslims in Rakhine State, Myanmar, is forcing people to migrate internationally. The Rohingya are now the world's largest stateless population.[28]

In my capacity as a water chair for the United Nations Educational, Scientific and Cultural Organization, I conducted fieldwork in 2019 at the Kutupalong Rohingya refugee camp. Flying into the Bangladeshi tourist resort town of Cox's Bazar, where the beaches are lined with high-rise hotels, children selling coconuts and fresh fruit cocktails, and some locals riding small horses along the edges of the sea, one would never guess that just a few hours away was one the world's largest refugee camps, housing nearly 1 million Rohingya. More than half of the camp's residents were children. They lived in slum conditions, alongside dirt ditches filled with sewage and trash, in makeshift housing made of tarpaulins held together with wooden structures. The wood was harvested from what used to be a dense and rich area of forest and an important elephant migration corridor between Bangladesh and Myanmar. Wood from the forest also fueled the hundreds of thousands of stoves throughout the camp.

There was a crushing sense of despondency amongst every person I met. In large part, this was the result of a toxic combination of post-traumatic stress disorder from having witnessed and fled mass murder and rape; living day to day without a sense of future; and life in a state of limbo at the mercy of the goodwill of the international community, aid agencies, and the government of the host country. Local resentment toward the refugees was acute, and it was the upshot of many factors: the sudden influx of aid organizations into small towns, which was driving up the cost of local goods and real estate; increased traffic along small rural dirt roads made for low-impact travel; the fall in wages because the refugees were willing to work off the books and for less money; the environmental costs of a large number of people suddenly clearing the forest and setting up an informal settlement; and the loss of habitat for the Asian elephants that once roamed wild in the Teknaf Wildlife Sanctuary and were subsequently forced into the camp and nearby village, where they would wreak havoc. Some of the refugees shared stories of relatives having been trampled by the elephants when they crossed the border.

The fifth human migration variable is environmental. Environmental degradation, climate change, and weather-related disasters are increasingly influencing internal, intraregional, and international migration flows. The roughly 1,900 natural disasters that occurred throughout 2019 resulted in an estimated 24.9 million new environmentally displaced persons spread over 140 countries.[29] People are either moving within their country of origin or they are permanently or temporarily relocating to another country. The United Nations estimates that from 2008 to 2016, weather-related disasters forcibly displaced on average of 21.5 million people each year.[30] That is, approximately forty-one people are displaced each minute of every day.

Dry corridors in the Global South as a result of extreme drought can quickly tip already economically vulnerable people over the edge and into extreme poverty. At particular risk are subsistence farmers. Drought conditions can kill off cattle and crops, leaving rural communities without livelihoods and on the brink of starvation. For instance, farmers in El Salvador, Guatemala, and Honduras lost 280,000 hectares of beans and maize to drought in 2018.[31] Migration in this context can become part of a larger sequence of migrations. The first migration is rural to urban, and then, as rural migrants from the Global South encounter difficulties finding work and establishing themselves in the cities, they are compelled to emigrate to the Global North.[32]

Anthropogenic climate change is also impacting food sources and habitats for all life on earth. From 1880 to 2019, the global surface temperature warmed 1.8°F, with the Arctic warming more quickly than the global mean.[33] More and more species are geographically shifting, or are shifting their migration ranges as the climate continues to warm. Land animals are moving, on average, more than ten miles per decade.[34] Most plants and small mammals cannot shift their geographic ranges quickly enough to adapt, and some, such as the monarch butterfly, rely primarily upon temperature signals for migration, hibernation, and reproduction.[35] By 2100, human activities are predicted to raise global mean temperatures an additional 2° to 9.7°F over 2012 temperatures.[36] The more species are driven to geographically redistribute, the more this will compromise people's food and water security, livelihoods, and economies. For example, as species change their migration ranges, businesses geared to outdoor recreational activities such as birdwatching and fishing are negatively impacted.

In addition, as species are forced to migrate with changes to the global climatic cycle, the productivity and carbon sequestration capacities of ecosystems are undermined in ways that "transcend single systems or dimensions, with feedbacks and linkages among multiple interacting spatial and temporal scales and through entire ecosystems, inclusive of humans."[37] One of the multiple spatial and temporal interactions that has resulted from warming temperatures is genetic jumbling across generations. For instance, as the Arctic warms, grizzly bears have become more common in the area, leading to grizzly–polar bear hybrids with black-ringed eyes, mainly white fur with patches of brown, and long, grizzlyish claws.[38] Some might argue that the emergence of new hybrid species can lead to genetic diversity; however, it often has the opposite effect, especially when it comes to native species. For instance, the genetic fitness of hybrid cutthroat–rainbow trout is weaker than that of the individual cutthroat and rainbow trout species, leading to up to a 50% decline in the animal's reproductivity.[39]

Human activities—pollution, land clearing, greenhouse gas emissions—also are prompting the migration of plant species. Many terrestrial plant species are precluded from penetrating new territories because the human modifications made to some landscapes are not conducive to plants moving, but plant migrations are nothing new. Scientists who study ancient fossil records have shown that previous climatic upheavals have resulted in rapid and extensive plant community crusades to more favorable climates. Studying the fossil pollen records of thirty tree species over a 16,000-year time period, scientists have shown that the velocity with which the trees migrated south equaled, and sometimes exceeded, the pace of climatic changes, with the more northern species being both more sensitive to climate change and more vulnerable than their southern tree communities to mortality from the biotic interactions they experienced, the farther south they traveled.[40] Paleoecological evidence demonstrates that migration, not evolutionary adaptation, is the primary means through which organisms respond to changes in the climate.

As in the distant past, if the climate changes enough, organisms will need to migrate or suffer extinction. With future climate change scenarios for this century estimated to occur ten to one hundred times faster than the rate of the last period of deglaciation on earth, the science warns us that unless human beings facilitate the migratory response of organisms, mass extinction is highly probable.[41] There are two reasons for this. First, many organisms do not have the capacity to redistribute themselves at the speed at which climate change is occurring. Second, human land use patterns such as deforestation, the expansion of urban areas, and agricultural activities result in the loss of habitats and feeding corridors for other-than-human species, hereby inhibiting their redistribution.[42]

It is not only human earthlings that are being dispersed across the earth because of myriad forms of human violence. As a result of human activities changing the world's climate and causing widespread environmental degradation, the earth's entire life system is undergoing massive redistribution.

{ 4 }

Air

THE WATER BIRDS HAD MIGRATED an awe-inspiring 15,000 miles north in just forty days, moving in an S-shaped pattern across the globe. They had traveled counterclockwise around the South Atlantic before shifting to a clockwise route around the North Atlantic.[1] Picking up the pace with a tailwind, they landed in late May at the same Icelandic breeding grounds they had used for generations, alongside shallow waters. Upon arrival, they discovered their old friends—puffins, red knots, brent geese, black-legged kittiwakes, northern fulmars, and white-tailed eagles—had dwindled in numbers. The great ice sheets of the Arctic were melting, its waters were warming, and industrial-scale fishing and ocean resource extraction were turning the sea infertile.

This year, many of the ground nests remained either empty or were filled with unhatched eggs. Some eggs managed to break through the one-month incubation period to release a baby bird. The chicks filled the air with persistent screams of starvation as hunger passed from their stomachs into their bones. For the unlucky ones, color eventually left their feathers, until only their down moved when the wind blew. Bereft parents scoured the shallow, light-filled waters of the bay in vain for three weeks, searching for small schooling fish and pelagic invertebrates to feed their young. They made due with insects instead. Their new-parent exuberance quickly faded with the meager fish supplies. Breeding outcomes this year were worse than the last, and it was time to chase the summer early.

These past months of largely unproductive yet animated courtship, nesting, mating, breeding, and feeding were coming to a close. The darkness of winter was descending across the headlands and black volcanic coastline. The endless light and mild sea weather that had filled the past two months at Breidafjordur Bay had begun to chill. It was then that the cacophony of the Arctic tern colony suddenly quieted.

The tern puffed out her feathers to insulate herself in preparation for the cool temperatures that lay ahead. She lifted her black-crested head, scanning the sky. Yearning for a clear, strong wind, she gauged airflow speed and direction. She stood silent amidst the hushed colony, which was collectively perched and poised for takeoff. Airborne, her long, thin, light gray pointed wings were clasped loosely above her back, the bony arches not quite touching. Squinting from the ocean winds and sensing the opportunity these presented her four-ounce body, she spread her thirty-inch wingspan to full capacity. Gliding toward the open seas, she sensed the cliffs along the Icelandic shores receding. Untethered, she was resolutely moving toward a North Atlantic oceanic stopover that lay off the coast of West Africa. Here, she would pause for up to twenty-five days before continuing on her journey. Upon passing over the equator, migration paths of the colony would split, with some preferring to trace the coast of South America rather than of Africa.[2]

These were lean times, and the prospect of feasting on a new seasonal supply of marine food in the marginal Antarctic ice zone saturated her half-filled stomach with excitement and anticipation. All grit and fortitude, she thrust toward the setting sun, changing altitude to maximize speed, reveling in the spaciousness of the skies. The breeze whipped in between where her quills gripped into the vibrant warmth of skin below. Losing heat through her chili-red beak and legs, she shivered ever so briefly. In a little over a month, she reached the Weddell Sea, where she relaxed in the brisk warmth of an Antarctic summer, replenishing her energy and strength before recommencing the journey north, where she would partake in the annual mating and breeding season all over again.

The Arctic tern (*Sterna paradisaea*) has the longest migration path of any bird, some flying nearly 50,000 miles a year, which when calculated over the course of its lifetime, equates to approximately three trips to the moon and back again. Working in sync with its family and friends, the bird uses its olfactory map and the earth's magnetic field to navigate up to 44,000 miles of ocean annually.[3] Maximizing the full force of the wind, gusts of air fill their wings, blowing them across the globe even as they sleep and eat. The simple experience of air complementing their outstretched wings elevates them into the cold nimbostratus clouds and onto the calmer skies of altocumulus clouds, where they continue drifting in the low to mid-altitudes of the troposphere.

The earth's atmosphere is consistently populated with migrating species of all types and sizes, from the flocked migrations of large water and land birds through to the brave and bold journeys taken in solitude by the likes of the tiny hummingbird, which prefers to go it alone to avoid drawing the attention of predators. Then there are the soaring heights taken by the Ruppell's griffon vulture as it passes through the lower layers of cumulus clouds on its way to the blue-gray altostratus clouds thickly blanketing the sky at 14,000 feet above sea level, before touching the bottom of the stratosphere at 37,000 feet. The air becomes colder and colder the higher and higher it goes, until the temperature switches direction in the stratosphere. Here, the higher it climbs the warmer it turns. Here, it shares the dry air with wispy white cirrus clouds, commercial jet aircraft, ozone gas, and the occasional madcap skydiving human adventurer, such as Felix Baumgartner. On October 14, 2012, Baumgartner broke the speed of sound when he jumped from a high-altitude balloon, entering the stratosphere at 127,851 feet and landing in the U.S. state of New Mexico.[4]

To speak of the atmosphere in terms of layers, however, is misleading. The barriers separating the troposphere, stratosphere, mesosphere, thermosphere, and exosphere from one another are less finite and more porous than is implied by the model of single, isolated spheres divided according to temperature ranges and distance from the surface of the earth. More sympoietic than autopoietic, the atmosphere is constituted through a rich recipe combining differing variations of air density, air pressure, argon, carbon dioxide, helium, hydrogen, krypton, methane, neon, nitrogen, oxygen, radiation, temperature, vapor, and water. It is a physical and

chemical potpourri characterized by "linkages, feedback, coopera-
tion, and synergistic behaviour."[5]

Beth Dempster offers an important and helpful heuristic distinction for thinking about the qualitative character of atmospheric processes as these relate to the seas and terrestrial life.
Together, these produce the conditions for planetary life that
the Gaia theory captures. As a sympoietic system, Gaia does not
have self-defined boundaries; it is "collectively produced...
homeorhetic, evolutionary, distributively controlled, unpredictable
and adaptive." This stands in contrast to an autopoietic system, which, she explains, has "self-defined boundaries," is "organi-
zationally closed... homeostatic, development oriented, centrally
controlled, predictable and efficient."[6] A sympoietic system such
as Gaia is best broached using what Donna Harraway boldly calls
"tentacular thinking." It involves "storytelling and fact telling; it is a
patterning of possible worlds and possible times, material-semiotic
worlds, gone, here, and yet to come."[7]

Gaia is a historical entity that manifests in all facets of earthling
existence, just as much as earthling beings and processes manifest
themselves in it. It is a process of common production and mutual
permutation that creatively endures through the many spaces and
times that make up reality, the actuality of which is partially
known and understood and the potentiality of which can be
glimpsed or hinted at in the vacillations of music, art, poetry, literature, philosophy, and scientific hypothesizing and testing. Gaia
harbors no hidden purpose, nor is it a moral entity with the power
to lay judgment. The expansiveness of Gaia is more a testimony to
its vibrant secularity than a belief in a transcendent supernatural
being.

As human beings ventured beyond the atmospheres encircling
the earth, the distance created prompted a more intimate understanding of our earthly existence. It was like a switch flipped in the
consciousness of human earthlings, provoking us to sit up and
take note. Our survival depends upon a solitary entity floating

amongst the barren landscapes populating the solar system. One ethical outcome of human space travel has been the manner in which it introduced a paradigm shift in our understanding of alterity. It dramatically changed how humans understand their relationship to the earth and themselves, and they began to recognize a state of mutual vulnerability. The earth's relative precarity as a solitary living entity amidst an infinite constellation of barren landscapes that populate the solar system drew attention to our own precarity. The pervasive view of independent individuals engaged in rational thinking was offset by an ontological paradox: our vulnerability arises from our own sense of human invulnerability.

We are all familiar with the analog images taken by astronauts from the different voyages into outer space. The first photo ever taken of the earth from space was by NASA scientist John T. Mengel, on March 7, 1946.[8] But it was the analog color snapshot now known as *Earthrise*, taken by William Anders aboard Apollo 8 on December 24, 1968, that captured the eco-imagination of a generation and has been reproduced ad infinitum ever since. The image is credited with inspiring the rise of the environmental movement and the first Earth Day, which took place sixteen months later, on April 22, 1970, and which 20 million people are estimated to have attended. Earth Day Network's president, Kathleen Rogers, writes that the image "became a blinding confirmation that our Earth, floating in a sea of stars, was vulnerable and needed protection."[9] The photograph depicts the dry gray-brown terrain of a barren moon dwarfing the colorful marble blues, whites, and oranges of earth suspended in the pitch-black darkness of space. The scientific objectivity of the photograph carries traces of the astronaut's awe-filled gaze, the singularity of that moment meeting the singularity of earth's irreducibility.

The images astronauts took aboard the Apollo voyages pricked the normative confidence in the power of human reason, technological invention, and ingenuity. The social, political, and cultural events of the time all reinforced the weakening of human self-assurance. It was a historical moment that re-presented catastrophe as immanent to the muscular rhetoric of triumphalism and civilizational progress in which both sides of the Cold War engaged. At the time, the world was gripped in a political and ideological struggle between capitalist democracies, under the umbrella of the United States, and Soviet-style communism characterizing the Union of Soviet Socialist Republics. At the center of this struggle was a frenzied nuclear arms race that threatened to blow the earth and everyone on it into oblivion.

Then arrived the Apollo images of earth taken from space. The images facilitated a new experience of the world, of its place in the solar system, and of our place in it. This was an experience grounded in an ethics of alterity and affect, or as Walter Benjamin put it in "A Short History of Photography" (1931), "Instead of a space worked through by a human consciousness there appears one which is affected unconsciously . . . Photography makes aware for the first time the optical unconscious, just as psychoanalysis discloses the instinctual unconscious."[10] When the Apollo earth images were publicly released, a trembling sense of awe and wonder was met with the terrifying realization that this earth is all we have. To preempt the rallying call of climate justice activists decades later, there is no planet B.

Viewed from the perspective of outer space, the power and fragility of a living earth as the only planet in the solar system (as far as we know) that has a protective outer layer that enables us to breathe easy and venture outdoors without being scorched by the sun's rays, and that maintains a livable surface temperature range conducive to the flourishing of a wide variety of life forms and ecosystems. Uniquely positioned at just the right distance from the sun to reach a Goldilocks balance—neither too hot nor too cold but just right—and support life on earth.

The Apollo and subsequent NASA images of the earth taken from space present us with a subject that returns our gaze by the sheer facticity that its vulnerability is something we hold in common. It is this realization of a shared vulnerability that holds us to account. Viewed from space, gazing back at us, the earth has no subjective interiority; it is neither vengeful, judgmental, nor brave. It simply states its existence and leaves the rest up to us to narrate.

More recently, Michael Benson has taken up the affective and ethical potential of the NASA photographic images. Benson's *Otherworlds* exhibit at the Natural History Museum in London presented images the human eye would see if traveling through space.[11] He takes the images of earth and the solar system and then reconstructs digital photographs of the solar system to create a series of images that together contextualize earthly existence. He begins with the numerous black-and-white analog and digital pictures robotic spacecraft have taken using red, blue, and green filters. He then works on these multiple sectional images by inserting them into an artistic feedback loop, excavating and treating the visual data to eventually create images the human eye can recognize, while also creating an auratic tension between intimacy and distance. Benjamin describes "aura" in photography as a "peculiar web of space and time: the unique manifestation of a distance, however near it may be."[12] Working as a visual craftsman, Benson builds new frames to fill in absent sections. If a red-, blue-, or green-filtered image is missing, he produces one. Each digital image is thus a composite of many images, the result of layering all the available visual data about single planets, moons, space objects, and comets. In short, it is through the interplay of actual and potential views of space exploration that Benson produces a singular narrative of the solar system.

What I find intriguing about Benson's method is the nonlinear additive process he uses. He is more interested in how perception is structured than in the subject perceived or the medium of perception. In this way, the form and content of his digital reworking of images from space present a poignant portrait of a living earth, an "afterimage" that creates an image the human eye can recognize and also an image in which we find our own reflection. The aura of unique atmosphere, water, and land that characterizes the earth clearly is absent on all the other space objects and planets he presents. The living system that is the earth is not reproduced anywhere else in the solar system. The resulting series of images is both a painterly representation and an interpretation of earthling existence. In effect, a tenuous uniqueness arises as earth's solar neighborhood is unearthed. Nothing out there in space even comes close to resembling Gaia, yet all that is out there is, in part, an ingredient of the collective existence that is the earth. The canyons, craters, infernos, fog, haze, rocks, anticyclonic storms, sunlight reflections, ice, and dust that make up the dreamlike darkness of the solar system accentuate, contextualize, and bring into relief the singularity that is the earth.

Viewed from space, the earth is constantly changing. There are all kinds of storm activity, clear skies and night skies, tornadoes, hurricanes, and more, all set against the backdrop of space. "From space," said Syrian astronaut Muhammad Ahmad Faris, "I saw Earth—indescribably beautiful with the scars of national boundaries gone."[13] Those few human beings who have blasted through all five layers of the atmosphere and have floated without gravity in the solar system, looking back at the earth, report an overpowering feeling and awe-inspiring experience. They speak of a radical shift in consciousness, or what Frank White calls the "overview effect."[14] As NASA astronaut Kathryn D. Sullivan describes it, "It's hard to explain how amazing and magical this experience is. First of all, there's the astounding beauty and diversity of the planet itself, scrolling across your view at what appears to be a smooth, stately pace . . . I'm happy to report that no amount of prior study or training can fully prepare anybody for the awe and wonder this inspires."[15]

The central principle at the heart of the concept of an overview effect is that of distance. From space, the singular reality of the earth comes into focus. David Yaden and his team studied the psychological impact on astronauts and cosmonauts of viewing the earth from outside of the earth's atmosphere. In addition to the more "socially and spatially inclusive language" the respondents used to describe their experience in space, the overview effect also prompted a profound sense of connectedness, imbuing in them a new, inclusive sense of care and responsibility toward all life, encompassing all "humankind, and even the entirety of existence." Indeed, it introduced a new way of studying the earth, eventually inspiring James Lovelock and Lynn Margulis to launch the idea of Gaia.

There is no one study of the earth. Rather, there exists experimentation, performance, questioning, and exploration, a survey of the many earthling movements amidst the multiple iterations of Gaia. Earthling science is an art of navigation, of discovering what connects the many earthlings that together create life, of examining Gaia up close and from afar and being willing to learn from both.

Studies of earthlings can never simply be a strictly scientific undertaking. This is because Gaia is both a science and a weltanschauung. It is an empirical and theoretical approach to the study of life, as much as it is a realistic and creative attitude toward life; it is an attitude that is comfortable working within and with paradox. As Bruno Latour summarizes it, Gaia helps you understand that "you can no longer distinguish between organisms and their environments."[16] It involves venturing into the murky realms of transpeciesist ethics, transgenerational affections, and transnational response-abilities. It demands that human beings take on how humanity works by keeping its species-specific perspective ajar so that other-than-human experiences, histories, agencies, and socialities can present with autonomy and integrity. It is an approach to study that involves lingering with curiosity and shuddering in discomfort, practicing impersonation, being under the influence yet always remaining alert, and refusing to be lulled into complacency or a false sense of security.

Earthling studies encompass many methodologies. It is a method of wayfinding through the smooth spaces of the ocean ahead of the firm ground of ideology, the liberal perspective of individual freedom, and the endless quest to discover the essence of things. It is a transenvironmental method that begins from a position of defiance by disrespecting the boundaries of disciplines, speciesism, generations, and citizenship. It is a method of creative production aimed at producing kaleidoscopic descriptions of the pure sciences as they are placed in conversation with the arts, humanities, and social sciences, infusing temporal differences with divergent spatial organizations and scales. This is a method of making, of braiding imagination with matter and memory, as Henri Bergson might have advocated.[17]

Latour has warned that studying the earth means undertaking a hyperactive course of study, one that complicates the disinterested positioning of an outside observer. In qualification of this claim, he explains that "with Gaia you are inside it while hearing the loud crashing of outside/inside boundaries."[18] It's like whirling and crunching your way up through the earth's crust, then crawling and scrambling across the ground into trees and over cities, prior to plunging into the waves, where you navigate the riptides before continuing on up into the atmosphere. Here, the solitude of space appears. You hold your breath ahead of gliding around the globe in exhilaration and admiration. Twisting and tumbling, you make a downward descent, landing squarely back on the surface of earth again, all exhausted and content. On land, gravity allows you to set your feet firmly on the ground. You remove the oxygen-filled vessel attached to your insulated space suit, that body armor which has kept you warm against the freezing temperatures of space. Now, in the quietness of it all, you slowly and deliberately fill your lungs with fresh air—the same air that warms all life on earth; the same air that gravity keeps from escaping into space; the same air that all breathing species need to survive.

Although all life on earth uses the same air, healthy, equitable access to it is unevenly distributed. The production of "airscapes," a term I am using to refer to the combination of air and the atmosphere, are infused with racial injustices and capital accumulation. Airscapes function as an effective means to realize surplus value the world over. Whether it is the estimated $215 billion value of the world's carbon market in 2019, the $828 billion global airline industry, or the slightly more than $7.5 billion that the U.S. Federal Communications Commission received from twenty-eight wireless providers for 3.4 gigahertz of U.S. airwaves, the world's airscapes are without doubt a lucrative industry.[19] The flip side to the economics of air comes into focus when we calculate, as the Center for Research on Energy and Clean Air has done, the financial burden of air pollution. In 2018, the global burning of oil, coal, and gas carried a $2.9 trillion price tag, or 3.3% of global gross domestic product, in increased health care costs and decreasing economic productivity. Global air pollution killed approximately 4.5 million people and was "responsible for 1.8 billion days of work absence, 4 million new cases of child asthma, and 2 million preterm births."[20]

Airscape disparities manifest in the ongoing deterioration of the atmosphere as more and more global warming emissions continue to endanger all future species; when Clean Air Act legislation is undermined and unraveled by special interest groups; when the buildup of nitrogen in the atmosphere from combustion byproducts associated with cars, trucks, and agricultural activities goes on to disrupt and compromise oceanic life; in the rampant deforestation that destroys both important carbon sinks and the trees cleaning the air of CO_2; and in the disproportionately polluted air breathed by the poor and by communities of color.[21] Social disparities, injustices, discrimination, and marginalization all linger and color the air we collectively breathe. So although air might be everywhere, it is unfairly shared. In the United States, the breathing of people of color is politicized and militarized, consciously impaired by law enforcement, who in seizing control of the air turn it into a lethal weapon they wield against Black and brown lives to choke them to death.[22]

Please.
Please.
Please, officer, I can't breathe!

And here it was again, another male Black body falling into disarray as the pressure from the white officer's knee chased the air straight from his chest. A sharp heat moved from the left side of his cheek, ending at his feet as his body was ground against the street. The cop persisted, and his buddies looked on, jeering and almost breaking into song. The asphalt sliced its way through the dark skin, spilling forth a racist unconscious of slavery and lynching.

The white officer knelt down hard, adjusting his pose on the nearly still body below. A smirk of formality streaked across his face before he briefly boasted,

If you can speak,
You can breathe.

In this gasping state, air struggled to reawaken the lungs of a man mere seconds from death, his last moments submerged with alarm under the weight of a white shibboleth. His eyes caught the horror-filled gaze of bystanders nearby. He pleaded for a witness. A witness to intervene. He prayed for his mama and begged not to die. Then his shrieks weakened and subsided. He had been asphyxiated. Nine minutes and twenty-nine seconds is all it took for a heartbeat to say good-bye.

And there it was. The long darkness of national Black hatred came billowing back from beyond the years of civil rights struggles for justice and equality, to a time when enslaved Black bodies hung and swung from trees because of an act of self-defense, for sitting while a white man stood, for a wrong look, for reading a book, or under the pretense of moral sense. There it was, a brief, wicked moment of venomous inhumanity repeating itself into infinity. A flash of cruelty, summed up in a flippant retort and malicious grin. An ice-cold moment of white privilege refusing to give in. The accusations used to justify homicide turned into a hollow list of threadbare lies in support of a crime: "Uncooperative," "Noncompliant," "Resisting arrest," "Erratic," "Agitated."

The repeated cries of "Please, officer, I can't breathe!" haunt the punched, kicked, beaten, shot, tased, and asphyxiated Black and brown bodies thrown underground and alone. Officer after officer walks free without accountability—uncharged, released, and acquitted for using deadly force in the name of civility.[23] Meanwhile, outrage and heartbreak rip through teargassed municipalities, inflamed and seething from the injustice of it all, demanding that history say their names:

George Floyd, Breonna Taylor, Ahmaud Arbery, Samuel DuBose, Billy Ray Davis, Trayvon Martin, Tamir Rice, Michael Brown, Eric Gardner, Quintonio LeGrier, Bettie Jones, Harith Augustus, Rekia Boyd, Philando Castile, Jamel Floyd, Keith Childress Jr., Michael Noel, Leroy Browning, Roy Nelson, Miguel Espinal, Tiara Thomas, Jamar Clark, Alonzo Smith, Lamontez Jones, Wayne Wheeler . . .

{ 5 }

Ocean

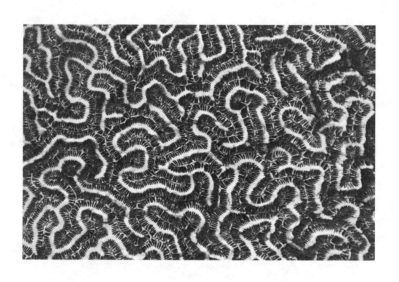

GROWING UP IN SYDNEY, AUSTRALIA, it was a rite of passage to learn how to self-reliantly navigate the unmannered surf with its unexpected currents. Understanding how to distinguish between lethal and benign sea creatures happened more by chance and wretched experience than by sitting behind a desk in a formalized classroom. Like the day the leg of a skinny, tanned kid met the piercing sting of a bluebottle jellyfish (*Physalia utriculus*). His high-pitched screams darted along the half-mile-long beach, causing people to abruptly sit erect on their towels to check out what the racket was all about. His freckle-faced friend was desperately urinating on the sting site. A swollen red line wrapped around his calf like a ruby necklace, the defensive imprint of the creature's tentacles. Clearly, the pee was far too alkaline, because it was causing the pain to intensify and the boy's cry to heighten into an earsplitting shrillness. The more the urine hit the injury, the more sting cells the wound discharged, until the child was shivering in pain.

The name bluebottle jellyfish is a misnomer. It isn't technically a jellyfish. It is a colony of four separate organisms, each with a specific function: floating, fishing for food, digesting, or reproducing (gonozooids). Its tentacle is formed into a long, bright, lazuline-blue thread that can reach up to 160 feet in length. The nematocyst, or stinger strand, is deceptively beautiful, elegantly undulating just below the surface of the sea. The animal is one of approximately 175 known siphonophore species that occupy the world's oceans.[1] Like other bioluminescent organisms, its glowing color is enriched when it becomes agitated. Each year, armadas of these small creatures are blown onto the beaches of Australia. Less frequently, a larger species of bluebottles with multiple stinging tentacles are seen up and down the country's East Coast. Envenoming by these jellyfish, as with the box jellyfish (*Carukia barnesi*), causes Irukandji syndrome, with symptoms such as vomiting and severe cardiac failure, sometimes resulting in death.[2] Luckily for the kid on the beach, this more uncommon species of bluebottle was not the one that had sunk its stinging capsules into his skin. Regard-less, it bloody hurt.

Impatient from the insistent heat and the uninterrupted shriek-ing of the stung kid, I took off in the opposite direction. With the sand burning the soles of my feet, I was keen to hit the water. Grubby with salt, sand, and sunscreen, I rushed toward the buck-ing waves, all gung ho and certain. As soon as the water hit waist height, I plunged into the saline lather, vigorously swimming toward the horizon line of the South Pacific, stopping about where the baited shark nets hung. Out there, beyond the commo-tion of tourists, teens, and surfies, the unmannered movement of the ocean subsided. I bobbed on my back, hypnotized by a blizzard of squawking gulls circling above. I drifted there, taking in the vastness of this blue planet we human beings call home.

For a long time, scientists hypothesized that water arrived via wet asteroids and ice-carrying comets after planet earth formed.[3] This theory presupposes that earth originally existed as a dry planet formed as a result of a high-energy collision. In addition, volca-nic activity released water-filled gases, helping to create the atmo-sphere, which eventually produced the rains that filled the dry crevices of the earth's crust and went on to form the oceans.[4] An alternative and more recent hypothesis for how earth got its water points to ancient meteorites, or carbonaceous chondrites, as the source. These are estimated to have been in existence around the time that the solar system formed, some 4.6 billion years ago, well before planets existed. As carbonaceous chondrites contain earthlike water, scientists now propose that earth may not only have received its water from them but that its water and rock formed concomitantly.[5]

The fluid oceanic space covering 70% of the earth's surface is in a continual state of circulation. Moving clockwise in the north and counterclockwise in the south, a total of 352 quintillion gallons of water is continually in motion, massaging, spinning, bouncing, and swinging over some 140 million square miles.[6] The abiotic movement of water occurs at different depths of the ocean, with salinity and temperature changes prompting a global ocean current system called the global conveyor belt. The conveyor moves cold, salty, dense water southward from the depths of the North Atlantic, past Africa and South America, where it swells and warms, onto and around the Antarctic, where it cools again before bifurcating into two warmer paths. One path leads past the Indian Ocean, the other, the Pacific. And there I was, in my seventy-six-pound teenage body, floating rudderless in an untangled solitude on that 107°F day, in water billions of years old as it passed through the Pacific Ocean on its thousand-year-long journey around the globe.

Suddenly, out of nowhere, the sea switched direction. I raised my arm, frantically waving to catch the lifeguard's attention, only to remember too late that I had entered the sea outside the flags. The lifeguard station was more than a quarter of a mile up the beach; the nearest lifeguard was clearly out of earshot, and too far north to notice me bobbing away down on the southernmost edge. The ocean currents stretched me out to sea. I was gasping for breath, but it was not air that entered my lungs; it was seawater. The rough waters had triumphed over my barely adult body. I was slipping in and out of the swells, unheralded, sinking farther and farther under the reflective aquamarine surface, into a space where my shadow disappeared. Mustering up all the strength I could, I made what seemed like one last effort to rise up. Once the sky reappeared, I flipped onto my back, arching it hard to remain afloat.

The number one lesson of any surfer caught in a rip is to humble your body before the formidable space. Allow it to take you out to sea until its byzantine movements eventually smooth and dissipate, and then swim around the localized current vigorously pushing you away from the beach. Only then is it possible to swim back to steady land. This lesson announced itself just in time. Choking, I eased my way out of the froth-filled swash as I neared the shore.

It must have been a half hour or so that I lay limp in the ebb and flow, calmed by its predictability. I was feeling faint but nonetheless relieved, until the smell of the warm sea breeze soothed me back to confidence. I nearly drowned that day.

My mind wandered up the coast to the Great Barrier Reef, to the thousands of corals suffering a different kind of brush with mortality in the ocean. Even then, the warm waters of a changing global climate were weakening and killing large sections of the ancient reefs, and the situation has continued to deteriorate. The coral bleaching event of 2016 impacted more than 60% of the coral in the northern Great Barrier Reef.[7] Under warm water conditions, the algae that coral depends upon grow distressed and exhausted, making the algae act erratically. With each aching pulse the algae radiate, the coral convulses, exhaling the algal symbionts from its tissue, eventually turning the coral white. Bleached coral is vulnerable, and if it is not given time to recuperate in cooler waters, it will die. It can take years for bleached coral to fully recover. As human activities continue to warm the global climate, the warming of tropical waters becomes more frequent and severe. Not only is there not enough time between bleaching events to allow the coral to mend, but also the water can become so hot that the coral dies suddenly, cooked by its own habitat.

Neither animal, mineral, nor plant, coral is a magical mixture of all three. Its polyp is an animal relative of the jellyfish and sea anemones; it is a mineral in the sense that the polyp uses seawater to build a strong limestone skeleton (calicle) to protect its fragile body; and it depends on forming a symbiotic relationship with plant algae for its survival. When microscopic polyp larvae fall onto the ocean substrate, they attach to a hard surface. Here, the polyp buds into thousands of clones that together form coral branches. The organism creates a colony by joining its skeleton to other, usually genetically identical, polyps. The collective combination of coral skeletons creates the reef structure that becomes an important habitat for small fish and marine life.

At night, the polyps use the nematocysts on their tentacles to kill, capture, and consume tiny marine life, such as zooplankton. The corals consume photosynthetic algae (zooxanthellae), which they need for their long-term survival, but rather than digesting these algae, they move them into their tissue, where the algae can continue living. The coral and the algae form a thriving symbiotic partnership, with the algae giving the coral its magnificent color and photosynthetic energy and the coral serving as the algae's host.

The Great Barrier Reef sits off the north coast of Queensland. It is a United Nations Educational, Scientific and Cultural Organization World Heritage site and one of the world's largest living reef ecosystems. People from around the world visit the area on a mission to witness the kaleidoscopic waters filled with captivating marine life and a breathtaking abundance of coral species, before all is lost to bleaching and climate change. From 2015 to 2016, reef visitors together generated a total asset value of $56 billion, adding $6.4 billion to the Australian economy and supporting 64,000 jobs.[8] Whether they are snorkeling, swimming, diving, peering through glass-bottomed boats, sailing the mild waters on a chartered yacht or catamaran, or catching a bird's-eye view from a helicopter or seaplane, people from across the globe, tempted by the reef, temporarily leave behind their two-dimensional existence of life on land and the gravitational pull that ties them to it. Here on the reef, *Homo sapiens* enters the three-dimensional existence of ocean life, "freed from the limitations of gravity," as James Lovelock has described it.[9] Equipped with cameras and other devices, humans set out to capture and consume the reciprocal evolution of life under the sea, partaking, albeit briefly, in the secular and fantastical immensity of Gaia's invention: the ocean.

Aboriginal and Torres Strait Islanders are the traditional owners of the Great Barrier Reef. For them, the marine environment is filled with creation stories of ancestral spirits, of a creator who, enraged by an insubordinate human, spewed lava and rock that later formed the reef. It is also home to ancestral burial areas and sacred sites and to a timeless cultural and emotional dreaming that is intimately tied to the environmental specificities that make up the north Australian coastal region. The stories of ancestral beings and the Dreamtime of the traditional folklore, music, and ceremony of Australia's First Peoples far exceeds the oft-quoted $56 billion price tag that is cited as the rationale for protecting the reef.[10] This is because, through story, song, dance, and art, Aboriginal and Torres Strait Islander communities celebrate, affirm, and reflect upon their Indigenous Australian identity. For the Torres Strait Islanders whose home is on the islands off the north coast of Australia, there is a politics tied to their reef-specific cultural practices, as these also provide an important means through which to resist their marginalization within both Australian society and the larger, mainland-based Indigenous Australian communities.[11]

Indeed, the tourist's experience of the reef as an environment to be captured on camera, a box to be checked off on a long inventory of bucket list items, and in turn a branding image of Australian identity that carries enormous value when commoditized on the free market, is in itself symptomatic of the limits of non-Indigenous ways of experiencing, knowing, and evaluating the value of the reef. The reef stories of the Dreamtime not only provide Australia's First Peoples with historical continuity; they also present a spiritual yet secular understanding of the oceans as constituted through a diversity of ubiquitous times that qualitatively shape the unique relationship they have with reef life. Their relationship has concrete implications that are manifested in sustainable land and water management strategies, oral knowledge of the medicinal properties of coastal flora and fauna, and distinct ceremonial domains.[12]

There was a time, quietly thought the sea, when the reef waters touched the corals as a lover in blind surrender, endlessly fondling its polyps with zooplankton and phytoplankton. The waters and coral were bound together in adoration and tenderness, their love flourished, and they wandered in to and out of ideal temperature ranges. Until one day, at the end of November 2014, El Niño visited the reef, recruiting the waters into its grip. Infidelity suddenly rose the water temperature by a dangerous 2°F. Convulsing with distress, the fragile *Acropora* colonies vomited up their brown-green zooxanthellae, turning the previously plump and spirited coral white with malnutrition and misery. Broken by the four-year-long betrayal, the corals longed for the temperate water to return.

Before the coral knew it, a herd of humans had descended, all poised and ready to walk the reef. The corals braced themselves, uneasily awaiting the onslaught. Then it began: human after human climbed down onto the reef. Drunk with delight at the prospect of reef play, they jumped for joy as they left the shore, eagerly trampling their way through the shallowest sections of the fringing reef colony. Their body weight destroyed the coral's skeletons. Its tentacles were grabbed as the unsteady terrestrial creatures lost their balance on the uneven ocean floor. Diver fins kicked and broke its branches, while younger humans, filled with curiosity, tore apart entire sections of the colony, overturning and inspecting the stony scleractinians. With its foundation compromised, the colony was knocked off balance. The *Acropora millepora* and the living tissue of the *Porites lutea* skeletons suffered the most from the ambush.[13] Fatigued, the corals lost their will to reproduce, holding back on releasing their gametes into the water; others abstained from brooding their tiny planula larvae altogether.

Defeated by capricious water temperatures and the unforgiving hostility of human behavior, the tattered reef lay limp and despondent, on the verge of giving up. Now forsaken by clemency, the once supple corals stared aghast into the reticent waters without a clue about what to do. Their structural complexity now compromised, the number of coral genera reduced, and abandoned by the fish that had once called this colony home, a solid silence moved across the water, stiffening the reef into compliance.

The remaining coral clutched the rocky base, yearning for the familiar temperature range to return. Acoustically dead, the reef ecosystem craved the resumption of the crunching, crackling, groaning sounds of healthy reef life.

Marine biologist Tim Gordon has found that acoustic enrichment can assist with reef recovery.[14] Gordon and his team discovered that the biological soundscape of a damaged reef turns eerily quiet, because the diversity of marine life is weakened as fish abandon a sick reef. Reef recovery not only depends upon water temperature stabilizing over an extended period of time; it also needs a flourishing marine ecosystem filled with diverse fish species—herbivores, detritivores, planktivores, and predatory piscivores. Gordon's experiments show that placing loudspeakers under water and playing the sounds of a healthy marine habitat doubles the number and variety of fish species returning to a reef. This is not to suggest that auditory augmentation provides a panacea to the destructive effect of climate change, but it does indicate that when used as one technique of conservation management, in conjunction with other conservation practices, it can support and enhance reef rehabilitation efforts.

The social life of the sea is constituted through a multiplicity of sound waves working at a variety of pitches, durations, and decibels, in addition to stretching across different spatial depths and breadths. Though our amphibious friends, such as dolphins, seals, and polar bears, enjoy listening both under and above water, the sounds of oceanic life are largely inaudible to the naked human ear. Even when human beings can hear underwater sounds, most marine life communicates in frequencies that sit outside of the average range of human hearing (20 to 20,000 hertz). This is because our auditory system is built to collect sound waves traveling through air conduction.

Vibration energy travels four times more quickly under water than in the air because particles remain closer together. Marine life has adapted its hearing mechanism to the manner in which sound energy travels through water by developing particle-motion acoustic abilities. Fish have three different hearing systems they use to perceive their fellow fish friends grunting and grating: cilia (nerve hairs), gas-filled bladders, and an accelerometer.[15] Although they are not as strong as fish in their hearing capabilities, prawns and cephalopods (octopods, squid, and cuttlefish) use a hair-filled sac, called a statocyst, to register sound pressure waves.[16]

On land, sound waves travel through the air. Air is more compressible than water, allowing pressure gradient energy to travel more effectively than particle motion through the air. Hence, human hearing has developed a pressure-sensing hearing mechanism. When sound waves vibrate through the air into the human outer ear, they travel to the middle ear, where the waves are amplified and their pressure is equalized before they move to the inner ear. There, the waves are transformed into electrical signals that move along the auditory nerve to the brain, which then registers the signals as sound. When humans are submerged under water, sound waves circumvent the outer and middle ear, traveling through bone conduction to the inner ear and muffling the quality of sound. Bone conduction under water allows humans to hear higher frequencies (sound waves moving up to 200,000 hertz per second) than they can with air conduction. That said, our best-quality hearing continues to sit within the range of human speech (500 to 3,000 hertz).[17]

The hearing capabilities of a bottlenose dolphin is much stronger than that of humans; their clicking sounds can reach up to 150 kilohertz, with a travel range of 328 feet to just under 2,000 feet. Odontocetes (toothed whales) rely on sounds they create to navigate their way through water. When in the water, they create sound waves that move through the water and bounce off of solids, creating an echo that returns to the sound-producing animal. The animal senses this in its jaw before the sound waves move into the inner ear. Odontocetes use this echolocation, or sonar as it is otherwise called, to communicate, feed, navigate, and orient themselves.[18]

In the 1970s, when Roger Payne, Scott McVay, and Katherine Payne first started their research on whale sounds, they placed underwater hydrophones to capture the enigmatic and wide range of sound wave frequencies that whales use. Most whale frequencies, especially at the lower end of the spectrum, fall outside the range of human hearing, with some of the lowest frequencies of a blue whale song falling as low as 16 hertz. Research shows that some whale songs (such as those of the blue whale and fin whale) can span an entire ocean, and that families in blue whale populations develop specific dialects. McVay and the Paynes also discovered that singing humpback whales repeat sounds and patterns to create music.[19]

In 1975, Greenpeace put the affective power of whale music to work as an activist tool, using it to both bring attention to and protest against the commercial whaling industry. A group of Greenpeace activists in inflatable boats put their lives on the line, confronting a Soviet whaling fleet of nine catcher boats and their mother ship, *Dalniy Vostok*, sixty miles off the coast of California. They challenged the crew with the sounds of whales absorbed in song.[20] The emotive potential of these large creatures serenading one another in the deep, dark depths of the sea, mixed with the evocative imagery of activists putting their bodies between hunters equipped with harpoons and their prey, raised international consciousness about the brutality of the whaling industry. Whales were being hunted to near extinction. In 1982, the International Whaling Commission banned deepwater whaling.[21]

Research on singing male humpback whales indicates that singing whales work together to create music. A recipient whale both repeats the monophonic melody line of the singer whale and introduces new melodic variations into its repetition of the melody.[22] Whales improvise with one another through compositional echoes, which at times overlap to form a polyphony of sound, using rhythm, duration, tone, timbre, and pitch. The sensation of disassembling and reassembling the melodies and rhythms of sounds arising from whale bodies swimming miles and miles away from each other points to an ethics rooted in the affective qualities of sound.

Reflecting upon the ethical implications of whale song in this way is not to assign an anthropocentric interpretation to whale behavior; rather, it is the opposite. Acknowledging that humpback whales' vocalizations are suggestive of an other-than-human ethic is to recognize ethics as, first and foremost, a capacity to care. In seeking companionship, the whales engage in transdependent sonic actions involving corporeal listening and performance. Theirs is a dynamic collective action of oceanic whale immersion. Whale singing skirts the exceptionalism of human morality, conveying instead a cooperative mode of bodily orientation in the sea that is contingent upon a contextualized connection to other bodies. Through a becoming oceanic—oscillating water molecules, pressure variation, sound energy, intensity, pressure, compression, particle acceleration and deceleration—the whales orient themselves in concert with the energetic materiality of the ocean reverberating through them. In this way, the great mammals of the sea affirm the indivisible quality of oceanic social life.

Given this intimate state of sonic co-constitution, it is unsurprising that anthropogenic acoustic disturbances in the oceans are having a debilitating and at times devastating impact on whales and other marine species.[23] The sounds of marine life are quickly being replaced by the noise of sonar mapping, remotely operated underwater vehicles, deep-sea mining, and more. After hundreds of years of land-based resource extraction, for instance, the seabed presents the next frontier for a mining industry that knows no limits, and the sound pollution this has introduced into the ocean is disrupting how marine life communicate, socialize, and find nourishment. Naval sonar so badly distresses beaked whales that they deliberately beach themselves, or they quickly seek the ocean depths, suffering microvascular hemorrhaging as their stressed bodies pressurize from diving too quickly.[24]

For centuries, the oceans have been used as a dumping ground for human-produced waste. The timeline of oceanic waste offers up important historical lessons on the ingenuity of human science and its limits. All manner of toxicity has, over time, been dumped there: radioactive waste from nuclear power plants and medical research; banned pesticides such as DDT; industrial waste containing acids, metals, and coal ash; dredged materials filled with cadmium, hydrocarbons, and mercury.

And let's not to forget plastics, which, depending on what form they take, may either release chemicals (bisphenol A, or BPA, as well as diethylhexyl phthalate, lead, cadmium, and mercury) or absorb toxins from other sources, contaminating the marine animals that ingest it. Each year, approximately 14 million tons of plastic end up in the world's oceans, much of which forms large floating plastic islands like the so-called Great Pacific Garbage Patch, which is larger than the state of Texas.[25] Marine biologist Matthew Savoca suggests that for some animals, such as seagulls, plastic smells like food, and there is the mounting challenge of dead, plastic-littered whale bodies turning up on beaches around the world. One theory holds that toothed whales that use echolocation to hunt ingest plastic because it sounds like food.[26] Plastics are designed not to biodegrade, so when marine animals become entangled in it, they drown. On the other hand, plastic provides a new habitat for some others, such as barnacles or mollusks. But one of the greatest challenges to the marine ecosystem is the amount of plastic ingested by marine life; one study estimated that this may amount to 12,000 to 24,000 tons per year.[27]

How far away is "far" for the ocean? How far out? How far down? And for all those creatures living along the ocean floor, how far up? The Challenger Deep in the Mariana Trench is the deepest stretch of ocean in the world. Located below the western Pacific Ocean, it is nearly seven miles deep, compared to an average ocean depth of 2.3 miles.[28] Advances in human technology toward the latter half of the twentieth century granted humans the means to journey into the depths of the Mariana Trench. In 1960, oceanographers Don Walsh and Jacques Piccard first visited there in a steel bathyscaphe designed by Piccard and his father. Half a century later, in 2012, filmmaker James Cameron followed their deep ocean descent. He documented in glorious detail the strange oceanic world he witnessed. Then again, in 2019, the explorer Victor Vescovo ventured there. One wonders what Vescovo saw from his submersible in the ink black depths of the sea. We do know, however, that swimming alongside those strange, translucent, and gelatinous creatures of the sea at a depth of 35,853 feet, in these frigid waters at the bottom of the ocean, was plastic![29]

Ecopreneur William McDonough and coauthor Michael Braungart point out, "Think about it: you may be referred to as a consumer, but there is very little that you actually consume—some food, some liquids. Everything else is designed for you to throw away when you are finished with it. But where is 'away'? Of course, 'away' does not really exist. 'Away' has gone away."[30]

As humans empty the oceans of its fish, capturing a total of 79.3 million tons of marine life in 2016 alone, the pollutants we and our ancestors have discarded into the sea return to fill our bodies with carcinogenic substances, microplastics, and toxicity.[31] The eternal return of Gaia keeps the ghostly remains of one species in motion until it eventually haunts another, pushing some organisms to uncannily reappear in others, and nudging inorganic matter to monstrously enhance and animate the biological potential of organic matter.

Loitering there, where the beach met the sea, I allowed grains of sand to groan between my toes and the salt to tingle-tangle the hairs on my skin. I had been determined to let my body win against the full force of a rip that was independent of human taming. I forever remember the day I let the ocean currents in, now fully aware how the sea strips bare the certainty that human arrogance can bring. Onward and over, and over again, swelled by the energy passed on from the wind, its waves frankly declare themselves to terrestrial earthlings: *Beware, and be not lulled into oblivion.* Here, the shipwrecked remains stuck to the seafloor strike a resonant chord, for without a moment's pause the sea may quickly change course, and in a twinkling it may travel from the serene to the severe and austere. For the ocean moves to the tempo of a disinterested truth of unconquerable frontiers of heat, moisture, and momentum, traversing a rotating sphere, steered by an energy exchange with the atmosphere.

*

{ 6 }

Ice

AS THE TIRED SUN COLLAPSED into the horizon and darkness thickened the air, the temperature dropped to just a few degrees above freezing. Twilight was drawing to a close earlier and earlier for every fall day that passed. Arctic life prepared for the immanent freeze. Seals and whales migrated south from the Beaufort Sea toward the Chukchi Sea across Barrow Canyon. Birds were in flight, moving around Point Barrow and through the Chukchi Corridor. In a little over an hour the radiant sky would be darkened. Solar winds carrying masses of electrically charged particles, discharged from the sun, were headed toward earth. In a few hours, some would enter the earth's atmosphere at the polar extremes, where the planet's magnetic field is weakest. There, inside the thermosphere, a gaseous collision of protons and electrons would burst with light and the pitch-black darkness of an Arctic night would suddenly become the backdrop for a series of luminescent green-and-pink-infused pirouettes. Aurora borealis was preparing to make an entrance.

Down on land, a seven-year-old mama polar bear (*Ursus maritimus*) found herself constrained to pacing the shoreline with her one-and-a-half-year-old cubs. She impatiently scanned the ocean, studying it for the familiar whiff of warm blubber. She decided to try her luck and reach what appeared to be an ice sheet floating a little offshore. There, her chances of catching a meal would improve. She slowly waded into the water, her two cubs close behind. She was a strong swimmer but she knew the cubs would need to quickly make their way to the floating ice, or return to land, to avoid drowning from exhaustion.[1]

Minutes later she was drifting waist deep in an ice slushy, her paws gripping onto remnants of frozen sheets. Moving crosswind, her moist black nose pointed to the sky, she tried her best to track the odor of fat-filled animals within a twenty-mile radius. The winds were too fast for her to follow the scent.[2] The ringed seals (*Pusa hispida*) were becoming harder and harder to hunt under these quasi-ice-free conditions.[3] She was slowly succumbing to the sour taste emaciation emits. The foam-filled edges of her mouth failed to extinguish the stress consuming her lethargic body.

Fatigued from the big swim, her two hungry cubs returned to land. They roamed the shore in starving confusion, raiding the nests of seabirds while their mother mined the waters for food. The ground beneath them had turned spongy from the massive melt taking place. Overcome with acute hunger, one of the cubs began shivering. Shivering turned into convulsions. Stunned, the brother of the tremor-filled cub frantically stood on his back two legs, head high, trying to locate their mother. All of a sudden, the stiffening and jerking muscle spasms of the starving cub stopped. Then the groaning sounds the baby animal released as air urgently pushed past his vocal cords quietened. His involuntary shaking came to a grinding halt. And now there was one polar cub. One polar cub, exposed on the shores of the southern Beaufort Sea, off the coast of Alaska.

The freeze was arriving late this year, pushing back the clock on the polar bear hunting season. The mother bear was exhausted from the vast distances she was compelled to swim in search of ringed seals. The changing ice habitat had already forced her to move her denning site to land. A year and a half later, the ice was rapidly retreating from the coastline again. For the summer months, this mama polar was forced to swim longer and longer distances before reaching ice stable and strong enough to carry her weight. All too often, it was over unproductive waters.

In more ice abundant years she had no problem sniffing out seal pups in their lairs, or slowly stalking them during the spring haulout, as they lay on the ice, shedding and replacing their skin and fur, or by simply standing in wait over breathing holes until they came up for air.[4] Hunting opportunities abounded on the old ice. The enlarged olfactory bulb in her brain equipped her with a keen sense of smell to find her prey in lairs up to three feet under the snow, or miles away. This expanded sense of smell, combined with a hearing range from 11,200 to 22,500 hertz, enabled her to refine the location of seals under water and in the snow.[5]

Typically, the mama polar bear would eagerly and resolutely wait by an *aglu*, as the Iñupiat call seal breathing holes, sniffing for a potential meal. She would patiently stand on all fours, frozen in anticipation of a small, plump animal swimming the salty waters below to raise its nose through the six-foot-deep hole. If a seal did appear, mama was ready to quickly thrust her long neck and small head down the ice hole, grabbing the seal's tiny cranium in her jaw and using her full mouth of thirty-four teeth to crunch through the wriggling animal's skull.[6] Should she make a catch, she would use the front row of incisors to tear away the rich blubber, leaving the rest behind.

All she needed was one seal to replenish her and her cub's energy and fat reserves for a few days. Experience had taught her it was just a matter of time before the seal would make its grand appearance; if it didn't surface for a gasp of air within forty-five minutes, it would drown. She stared intently down the hole, with her four paws firmly placed on the ice for optimum balance. Finally, the water faintly gurgled, a sign of a seal breathing below. She dove her head hard and fast, but by the time she hit water the seal was long gone. She had miscalculated. The 140-pound animal had released a series of air bubbles to test and taunt potential polar predators waiting above the breathing hole. The tease had paid off and spared him his life. He continued on his way, foraging for Arctic cod and planktonic crustaceans.

Her energy level now low, mama decided to join her cub on land. Together they would scour the coastline for carcasses of bowhead whales (*Balaena mysticetus*) that Iñupiat hunters might have left behind.[7] An hour later, she and her cub were reunited, but it was short-lived. A ravenous male polar bear suddenly appeared. Panic-stricken, the mother dashed at full speed, her cub struggling to keep close. She came to a screaming halt, turned, then faced the approaching male. It was hopeless. He weighed eight hundred pounds compared to her 425, and his extremely low fat reserves were at a tipping point, making him particularly confrontational and belligerent. He needed to eat. In a matter of moments, her cub satisfied his shrinking stomach.

The scene took place just 668 miles from the small Iñupiat town of Shishmaref. It was October.

From 2001 to 2006, a mere 43% of Beaufort Sea polar bear cubs lived beyond a year, compared to a 65% one-year survival rate from the early 1980s to the mid-1990s.[8] Climate change is dramatically altering the animals' habitat, making polar cubs nutritionally distressed, such that their overall survival rates are plummeting. However, it is not only the polar bear populations that are suffering and migrating as the volume and extent of ice in the Northern Hemisphere changes. Many other species are doing so as well: whales (gray, bowhead, and beluga), Pacific walruses, seals (bearded, ribbon, ringed, and spotted), migratory birds, thirty-two documented fish species, and 174 documented invertebrate species.[9]

The frozen waters of the earth's cryosphere are dramatically changing as the climate warms and the movement of thermal energy around the globe shifts. The term *cryosphere*, derived from the Greek *kryo*, meaning "cold," refers to areas of the earth where water is frozen into sea ice, glaciers, snow, shelf ice, permafrost, lake ice, and river ice. As the earth's climate continues to warm, the duration, extent, and thickness of sea ice have all been impacted, disrupting sensitive cryospheric ecologies and rain and snowfall patterns. The frozen waters of the cryosphere also insulate the earth by reflecting approximately 80% of solar radiation back into space. By comparison, open waters reflect a mere 6% of the sun's rays and absorb approximately 90% of them. For this reason, the cryosphere plays an important role in incorporating fluctuations in the climate.[10]

Unsurprisingly, the changes occurring within the cryosphere serve as a valuable indicator of climate change. Old sea ice exists in the polar regions of the earth. Both poles are warming at a faster rate than are the lower latitudes. Relative to the average temperature for the period 1971 to 1999, Alaska was on the way to being 2° to 4°F higher by 2050 and 8° to 9°F higher by 2100.[11] In the Arctic from 2001 to 2013, September sea ice declined by nearly 25%.[12] The situation of Arctic sea ice is so dire that scientists predict the month of September will be completely ice free by the close of the twenty-first century, with some even estimating that this will occur between 2041 and 2060.[13] Meanwhile, satellite records show that from 2014 to 2017 Antarctic sea ice began rapidly decreasing in extent, moving at a pace that surpasses the rate of sea ice decline in the Arctic.[14]

Comparisons of 1988 and 2018 sea ice concentrations off the coast of Alaska show a dramatic decrease in the Chukchi and Beaufort Seas, with longer periods of open water, ranging from three to four months. Moreover, as the average temperatures of the Arctic warmed twice as fast as the rest of the earth, spring and summer Arctic snow cover declined at a faster rate than did sea ice.[15] This is important because snow insulates the ice from the atmosphere and it is essential to the process of ice formation. Sea ice is brighter and more reflective when it is covered with snow. The less snow coverage sea ice has, the more solar radiation it absorbs, further intensifying melting.

Overall, periods of open water in the Arctic are becoming longer and larger. The more open ocean waters there are, the more solar radiation the oceans absorb; this is albedo feedback. The resulting warmer waters transfer more heat to the atmosphere because the insulation that the sea ice provides between the cold atmosphere and warm water is compromised (conduction feedback), making the atmosphere layer more moist (cloud-ice feedback). All of this contributes to a warming climate. A warmer climate in turn reinforces this cycle, prompting further sea ice melt, releasing more warmth back into the atmosphere, accelerating global climatic warming, and impacting weather patterns. This feedback loop is referred to as polar or Arctic amplification, and it is why the Arctic is warming at twice the rate of lower latitudes.[16]

Seasonal sea ice loss in the Arctic affects the circulation systems of the ocean and atmosphere. For instance, the extra heat Arctic sea ice melt adds to the oceans and atmosphere alters the global jet stream air current. The jet stream moves storm activity around in the Northern Hemisphere and strengthens the trade winds of the Central Pacific.[17] The slowing of the jet stream from winter Arctic warming could explain the intensification of winter storms in North America and Europe in 2018–2019, and more extreme summer weather patterns in midlatitude regions.[18] Ocean salinity and temperature also change the density of oceanic waters. Cold and salty waters are more dense than warmer, less salty water. As the cryosphere melts, freshwater enters the ocean, making it denser and potentially more difficult for ocean water in the Arctic to sink and keep the global conveyor belt in motion.

The movement of seawater around the globe depends upon the warmer water of the equator traveling north on the surface of the ocean, up to the Arctic, where it is cooled, emits heat into the atmosphere, sinks, and then draws additional warmer water from the south. The great ocean conveyor, or thermohaline circulation, is a global circulatory mechanism. It remains in motion as new warm water enters, is cooled, emits heat, sinks, and again pulls in new warm water, contributing to the densification, and by extension the distribution, of ocean water around the globe. As the dense water falls to the bottom of the Arctic, nutrient-rich water at the bottom is pushed upward, providing an important source of sustenance in the spring growth cycle of phytoplankton, which feeds Arctic fish, birds, and whales.

Furthermore, the grooves and wedges characteristic of cryospheric permafrost landforms in the Arctic are thawing. Permafrost, or ground that has remained frozen for at least two years, covers approximately 25% of the Northern Hemisphere's exposed land surface and is typically found in high-altitude or high-latitude areas of the earth.[19] Thousands of years of frozen organic matter have built up in permafrost zones and remain stored in the earth's permafrost. However, as the ground thaws, the frozen organic carbon stored there begins to break down, presenting a risk of climate-warming greenhouse gases such as carbon dioxide and methane being released into the atmosphere and accelerating climate warming.[20]

Scientists have estimated that "permafrost soils will release between 68 and 508 Pg [petagrams of] carbon by 2100," and that the "additional surface warming generated by the feedback between permafrost carbon and climate is independent of the pathway of anthropogenic emissions followed in the twenty-first century."[21] As temperatures warm, the soil layer above permafrost areas, an area that seasonally freezes and thaws, slowly starts infiltrating the frozen ground below, and a permafrost carbon feedback loop kicks in.[22] The more the top layer of soil permeates the permafrost layer, the harder it is for the upper layer of soil to freeze when temperatures drop, further amplifying permafrost ice melt. Working Group 1 of the 2007 Intergovernmental Panel on Climate Change report noted that the temperature of the soil layer above the permafrost in the Arctic has increased by up to 3°C since the 1980s. These authors also noted that, from 1993 to 2003, changes to the cryosphere were responsible for a sea-level rise of 0.8 to 1.66 millimeters per year.[23] In addition to being a cause of global climate change, the loss of permafrost destabilizes the ground, triggering subsidence, landslides, and erosion.

The Alaskan town of Shishmaref, situated on a sliver of land called Sarichef Island, is disappearing into the Chukchi Sea because of both sea ice melt and permafrost thawing. The sea ice has historically provided the island community with an important protective barrier from severe weather. Now that warmer surface temperatures are causing permafrost retreat, the land on which the town of Shishmaref was built is becoming less stable. This, along with intense storm activity pounding an ice-free coastline, is leading to extensive erosion along the edges of the island, prompting large chunks of land and the village to slide into the sea. For instance, in just thirty-five years, from 1980 to 2015, Sarichef Island lost nearly 3,000 feet of land to the rising seas, increasingly frequent and intense storm activity, permafrost melt, and the coastal erosion that results from all three.[24]

As the character of the sea ice changes, so too do the Arctic ecologies sustaining animal and plant life on, in, and below the ice. The ice serves as both a source of food and a habitat. There are three primary effects associated with changes to the Arctic sea ice. The first is direct, such as polar bear starvation. The second, indirect, such as coastal erosion. And third, there are compound effects, namely the many feedback loops climate change sets in play. Climate change is also placing the biotic and physical world of the Arctic under stress, increasing the risk of an extinction domino effect coming into play as entire ecosystems are threatened with collapse.[25] Scientists report mortality increases amongst harp and ringed seal pups; new species invading the region; and earlier blooming of phytoplankton, a key ingredient in the flourishing of the Arctic marine food web, which no longer aligns with the eating cycles of marine life. Copepods eat the algae in Arctic waters, fish eat the copepods, seals eat the fish, polar bears eat the seals, and humans consume both fish and seals.[26]

For the Iñupiat of Sarichef Island, average temperature increases are slowly turning their traditional diet into a speciality. The decline in Arctic mammal populations, for example, means that the previously healthy, nutritious, affordable traditional food that Alaska natives sourced from the oceans, rivers, and mainland vegetation is gradually being abandoned. The Iñupiat of Shishmaref now primarily cook with prepackaged and canned goods purchased at the Nayokpuk General Store or the Shishmaref Native Store. As shopping replaces fishing, hunting, and gathering, household food budgets escalate and illnesses commonly associated with a diet high in fat and processed foods, such as cancer, diabetes, obesity, and tooth decay, become more widespread.

Climate warming sets in play mutually reinforcing patterns and affective states occurring across multiple scales and durations. The repetition of anthropocentrically triggered climate feedback loops are not a reductively closed system; they are open and continually mutating, altering the material specificities that constitute them as they morph. Repetition, in this context, produces difference; it does not reinforce the same conditions. It is a process of spatial, temporal, material, energetic repetition that differentiates and intensifies in its connection, an idea central to Gilles Deleuze's view of "difference in itself."[27] In this view, the process of variation contains within its formation the potential to actualize additional variations, much like the life system James Lovelock and Lynn Margulis describe with the theory of Gaia. Gaia, too, comprises specific entities that both create and undergo change as they differentiate in their connection. Gaia is an ongoing process of creative actualization. What this means in concrete terms is that it is unviable to isolate specific phenomenon and processes from their relational context without impacting both. (This idea will be central to my discussion of solastalgia in the era of ecological collapse, in chapter 7).

There is one direct action humans can take to stop global climate warming: end the burning of fossil fuels. The road to actualizing the ecological potential of this rather straightforward and almost naive claim, however, is far from simple. Decades of international climate talks beset by political obstructionism and cynicism eventually culminated in 197 signatories adopting the nonbinding 2015 Paris Agreement on climate.[28] A little less than a year after ratifying the agreement, however, the United States began the process of withdrawing from it. Fast-forward to September 2021 and six of the 197 signatories of the much-celebrated agreement still had not ratified it.

In 2019, Fundación Ecológica Universal reported "at least 130 nations, including 4 of the top 5 world's largest emitters, are falling short of contributing to meeting the 50% global emission reductions required by 2030 to limit the global temperature increase of 1.5°C above pre-industrial levels."[29] It may not be a foregone conclusion that the world will surpass the ecological tipping point of 2°C of warming above pre-industrial levels, but one thing is for certain: humanity is at an ecological crossroads. The entire basis for global ecological viability and flourishing, ours included, is now on the line.

In 2017, in my capacity as a UNESCO water chair, I spent time with the Iñupiat at Shishmaref, learning how the changing interface between water and climate was affecting their lives. I and my colleagues Jon and Sean Hughes documented stories of environmental change and the impact this is having on traditional ways of life.[30] I spent several days out on the ice, sometimes traveling on the back of a snowmobile with a young Iñupiat boy who drove like a bat out of hell from one family fishing hole to the next. Fishing was nothing fancy, just a simple piece of nylon line with bait on a hook dropped through a hole in the ice. The ice on the side of the island where the Arctic Lagoon meets the Shishmaref Inlet was made up of a vast network of fishing holes that families regularly tended, to ensure they wouldn't ice over.

Late in the afternoon and in early evening, I spent time in a kitchen or living room with extended families as they cooked up caribou, musk ox, and fish. Or I might be out on the front step, where the freezing winds made my teeth chatter and my hands turn blue, while the man of the house stood in the subzero temperatures with nothing more than a hoodie and jeans, brazenly cooking up burgers and hot dogs he had bought at the local store.

During the day, I visited with community leaders, including the mayor. She relayed a story about her uncle, who had disappeared out to sea, floating on a piece of ice that had detached itself from the mainland, surviving on raw meat torn from the carcass of his husky and by melting pieces of ice with his breath. He remained adrift like this in the midst of the Chukchi Sea for two weeks.

The mayor also shared with me that her uncle had been one of the luckier ones; others had disappeared completely.

"Your strength. Yes, it's your strength I fell in love with." Vincent Ningeulook lifted Ester's lowered chin, raising her downcast, blizzard-black eyes to meet his. He slowly nudged her pale wintergreen wool knit cap back from her forehead; a few strands of thick dark hair fell loose. She had collapsed, knees to her chest, her cheeks tearstained. She was giving up. The storm-filled waters engulfing vast sections of the tiny strip of land called Sarichef Island were robbing the inhabitants of their memories and restraining their dreams. This time, the raging gale winds had awoken the sleepy waters of the Chukchi Sea, pummeling Vincent and Ester's tiny two-bedroom home at the edge of Shishmaref village. This home was now precariously perched on the side of a cliff face.

The structure of their modest but much-loved house had collapsed under the sheer force of lightning, wind, and rain. It then began sliding down the slope as the firm ground beneath it disintegrated. Now unsteadily clutching the loose soil, half on land, half in water, the dwelling was on the brink of vanishing into the sea. The storm had huffed and it had puffed until it had blown their flimsy wooden home in.

Sixty-two-year-old Vincent was doing his best to coax his grief-stricken wife with steadfast hope. "We will rise, rebuild, and return to life as we know it," he tenderly reassured her. He leaned in, close enough to catch the scent of her body oils: lavender with a touch of mint. His eyes quietly searched for hers. But she refused his gaze. She knew better.

Just last fall their son Esau, rest his soul, had disappeared below the frozen waters. A deceptive blue ice, which generations of Iñupiat learning had found to be an indicator of thick ice, had turned unreliable. The flippant seasons had thinned the ice early. Thick and thin combined like a patchwork quilt tossed across the sea, impossible to read, deadly to misread. Blue ice or white ice? That was no longer the question, for the color differentiation no longer held sway. Both thick and thin sea ice had turned blue.

Hauling his seal hunting gear, Esau's huskies had dragged the heavy wooden *qamutik* (sled) across the ice in preparation for an extended spring hunting season. Two hours in and a low, guttural sound began reverberating over half a mile of the ice. It was the sound of fracturing sea ice mixing with the growling cries of Esau's spirit leaving his body. The unseasonably thin sea ice was breaking early. In an instant, Esau joined his ancestors in the freezing depths of the Chukchi Sea.[31]

Ester refused Vincent's reassuring glance because this was not a time to be tempted by the hubris of human foolishness. Instead, she chose to call upon the *anirniq* (spirits) and seek their guidance. The time had come to slowly pour melted snow into the mouth of a freshly killed seal and appease the fury of the *anirniq*. She had roused a shared Iñupiat ecological consciousness that went back multiple generations, a consciousness that realigned her humanity with reverence for the spirit of the caribou whose hair and skin warmed hers; the spirit of the *ugruk* (bearded seal) whose skin she sewed into *mukluk*s (boots) that her husband now wore and whose oil once fueled the *qulliq* (cooking lamp) her *ahna* (grandmother) used for cooking and warmth; the spirit of the wolf whose fur thawed her freezing hands; the spirit of the raw saffron cod her family ate to appease their hunger; and all the other living beings that had given their lives to sustain them.[32]

How to honor the love that bloomed in her memory of Esau? By offering thanks to the spirit wonder glowing throughout the world, and to the many more spirit strangers animating it, to the spirits who would bring in tomorrow, and to those changing the seasons and spanning time. For this she was thankful. The morning would come again. It might not bring with it the same life they had known for decades, even generations, but it was a life nonetheless. This simple but thunderous thought filled her with the strength to let joy in.

Rejected by her trustworthy eyes, overruled by the uncertainty of stormy skies, Vincent struggled to choke back the impulse to scream, to shout out against the injustice of it all. Instead, he made a choice. He refused to allow the shame of crying control him. The sobs hollowed his heart into what seemed like an eternal darkness. His piercing wail retrieved a long-gone sense of clarity for Ester.

She leaned into his chest, slipping her hand into his, and announced, "We must move to the mainland."

{ 7 }

Animalia

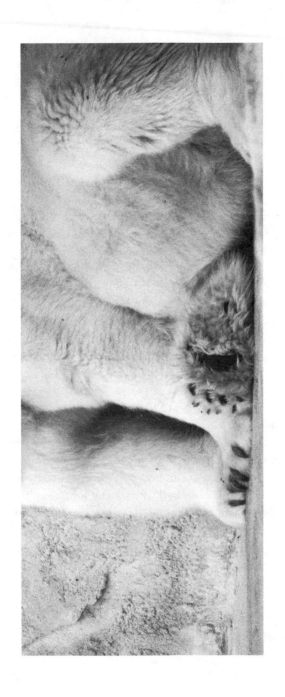

> As with every bottomless gaze, as with the eyes of the other, the gaze called "animal" offers to my sight the abyssal limit of the human: the inhuman or the ahuman, the ends of man, that is to say, the bordercrossing from which vantage man dares to announce himself to himself, thereby calling himself by the name that he believes he gives himself.
>
> —JACQUES DERRIDA, *THE ANIMAL THAT THEREFORE I AM*

THE SELFIE IMAGES FAILED to capture an animated moment made up of twitching muscles, a head rhythmically swaying from side to side, the lingering stench of stale marine meat fused with the sour pungent smell of piss puddles, the bold aromas of durian-flavored candy hitting salt-invigorated gustatory cells that had only seconds ago been saturated with vegetables pickled in brine, skin stretching tight and taut across a grinning face, thousands of nerves pulsating to the motion of a fluid-filled cochlea dancing to the high-pitched shouts delighted children make, along with a pupil constricting in reaction to photoreceptors suddenly satiated with bright light amidst the darkness. The resulting smartphone self-portraits swiftly circulated through the smooth spaces of cyberspace, pushed along by social media clicks and taps.

What the proliferating likes, cares, loves, and shares held in common was the manner in which they conjoined the quivering body of a distressed polar bear cub with the posturing body of a human-animal hollowed of empathy for the cub's suffering state. When taken together, the selfie images had turned a critical eye on the inhumanity of humanity. In effect, humanity was at a standstill—shorn of shame and consumed by self-absorbed grandiosity. Empathy had acquiesced to the aggressive emptiness of narcissistic exhibitionism.[1]

Pizza, the three-year-old polar bear, was pacing the 430-square-foot glass enclosure in an amusement park inside the Grandview shopping mall in Guangzhou City, China. Day in and day out the animal circled the same path along the rim of a shallow pool, momentarily pausing at a grate in the wall to try his luck again at clawing out of this shithole in which he had been dumped. Defeated by the uselessness of attempting any kind of breakout, he rocked his way past the artificial Arctic wall scene, through a patch of honey-flavored melting snow, before beginning the same routine all over again.

In this tightly temperature-controlled environment, the changing scent of salty air, frozen seascapes, oscillating skies, and wildlife were nonexistent. In their place was the whooshing hum of a mechanical system circulating air throughout the mall. The only thing that fluctuated each day was the blurred scenery of hands tapping on the glass display wall, the bursting lights of cameras, and the muffled noises of game halls.

Despite its Latin name, *Ursus maritimus*, this sea bear would never encounter the thrill and satisfaction of finding live prey out on old ice. The gurgling water two feet below the freeze, an indicator of a potential meal surfacing through an ice hole, had been replaced with a concrete replica of a hole. Whiskers designed to twitch to the smell of fresh seal blubber were sobered by the monotony of stale meat thrown through a wall chute. The hollow white hairs evolution had designed to transform the sun's ultraviolet rays into body heat were now prevented from participating in the natural wonder of polar–solar energy capture distinctive to this species.[2] The unchanging circumstances had wrecked Pizza's utility to the point that his thick fur was merely ornamental.

The barely polar polar bear had been subjected to an endless barrage of eager mall consumers who used his distressed image as a backdrop for a quick selfie before moving on to the belugas swimming in the filthy water next door. Confined to an area without sources of enrichment, the distressed cub was reduced to an impoverished version of himself, endlessly confused by the whimpering sounds his body continually made. Distraught with boredom and tortured by the decontextualized condition into which he had been thrust, he resorted to passing the time by repeatedly strutting from one corner of the tiny enclosure to the next.

The "prisonquarium" in southern China held all manner of species captive, from the beluga whales to the seven spotted seals fed by visitors, two sea lions anxiously rubbing their snouts along the bottom of a pool, a walrus in a two-meter-deep swimming area, and two limp Alaskan malamutes. And let's not forget the fish-filled display once occupied by a whale shark who never survived the trauma of being inserted into such a petrifying situation as that on offer at Grandview Mall Ocean World. Here, people could shop to their heart's content, become engrossed in video games, and make a detour through the center of the mall to take a quick selfie alongside a variety of other-than-human marine attractions.[3]

The ghoulish self-imaging alongside suffering as a source of entertainment and consumption offers three tiers of interpretation. First, the very act of gleefully imaging suffering as a source of one's own self-realization is a symbolic response to the current historical moment, to the dysfunctional relationship human-animals have with their ecological context and with other-than-human species. Second, it divulges the generalized state that nearly 1 trillion species on earth are experiencing, human-animals included, in their struggle to survive the concrete effects of inhumanity.[4] And last but not least, it renders intelligible the exploitative and oppressive system of global capitalism, which has resulted in a deeply decontextualized mode of existence.

In 2016, images of Pizza's tormented state spread throughout social media, prompting a public outcry. The anger of animal welfare groups was loud and influential. This is how Pizza was bestowed with the title of "saddest polar bear in the world."[5] Is this sadness an ethical demand that casts a spotlight on a long history of human violence waged against other-than-human animals? What constitutes the sadness to which animal rights activists refer? Does it denote the singularity of a life lost in the thrill of somebody else's selfie? Is this sadness a signpost directed toward the horrific realization that what we are witnessing with Pizza is both the specific life of an individual animal and life in general, a species of earthlings that has in many respects already vanished, and thus a dual vanishing arising from a fundamental failure on the part of humanity? Does it describe an animal spirit wilted by captivity? Specifically, Pizza was suffering from place-based distress: solastalgia.

Staring into the vanity mirror of inhumanity, the human animal is perched at the precipice of collapsing ecosystems and damaged habitats. Here, the forbidding loneliness of solastalgia appears. When support environments are severely damaged, a heightened sense of collective disempowerment can set in, which philosopher Glenn Albrecht has called solastalgia. Albrecht's "psychoterratic" focus shares affinities with many thinkers to whom he openly pays homage, from Aldo Leopold to Gregory Bateson to Rachel Carson and the even more recent ecogrief work of Phyllis Windle.[6]

In his ethnographic work on drought-afflicted communities and the coal mining communities along the Upper Hunter Region of New South Wales, Australia, Albrecht repeatedly discovered critical examples of suffering in response to damaged home environments. He describes this kind of distress as a psychoterratic illness, an "earth-related mental illness where people's mental well-being (psyche) is threatened by the severing of 'healthy' links between themselves and their home/territory."[7] In order to capture the grieving character of this place-based dynamic, Albrecht combined the experience of nostalgia with the idea of solace to create the neologism: *solastalgia*.

The word *nostalgia* derives from the Greek *nostos* (return home) and *algia* (pain). *Solace*, meanwhile, relates to the capacity to experience consolation under distressing circumstances. While solastalgia denotes a painful people–place relationship, similar to the way that nostalgia does, it is not premised upon the same idea of spatiotemporal estrangement from one's homeland, whether real or imagined, that nostalgia indicates. For example, the homesickness diasporic communities experience for a land they left could be described as nostalgia, not solastalgia.

Svetlana Boym formulates a helpful distinction between restorative and reflective experiences of nostalgia. The former, she says, "stresses *nostos* and attempts a transhistorical reconstruction of the lost home" and does not "think of itself as nostalgia, but rather as truth and tradition," protecting "absolute truth." The latter, however, "thrives in *algia*, the longing itself, and delays the homecoming— wistfully, ironically, desperately," dwelling on the "ambivalence of human longing and belonging," calling into doubt absolute truth.[8]

Another form of nostalgia that Boym describes is the yearning to prolong a lost time. Many cultural and philosophical figures of the nineteenth century experienced this type of nostalgia with the onset of modernity. As modern urban life replaced intimate traditional communities, many modern cultural figures held an ambivalent relationship to modernity. From Charles Baudelaire to Fyodor Dostoevsky, the sociologist Georg Simmel, and Walter Benjamin, Boym provides an excellent analysis of this tension between modernization and tradition as central to the nostalgic experience of modernity in nineteenth-century literature, art, and philosophy.[9] All these different kinds of nostalgic experience are related to, yet distinct from, the loss and pain associated with environmental devastation that solastalgia indicates.

In the communities Albrecht studied, people were neither pining for a long-lost homeland, in the way that an immigrant might, nor yearning for a traditional or perfect past now lost to time. Rather, they had become distressed by the devastation of a home environment for which they held a deep attachment and where they continued to live. Solastalgia, Albrecht insists, is "essentially an existential emotion tied to the lived human psychological relationship to land, place, home, 'country,' etc." Hence, solastalgia is a reciprocal person–place relationship: when a person's support environment is wrecked, their emotional and mental well-being is concomitantly impacted. Albrecht directly correlates a "person's biophysical location (place)" to a person's "states of health (physical or mental)."[10] He maintains that this is a specifically human condition, whereby dramatic change to an environment to which a person holds deep attachments not only impedes their ability to draw comfort from their context but also negatively impacts their sense of identity.

A logical inconsistency arises in how Albrecht constructs the concept of solastalgia, for it incorporates opposing philosophical views of anthropocentrically constructed subjectivity: materialist and immaterialist. The former follows a creative logic, the latter a negative one. The materialist destabilizes the notion of a fully bounded subject, asserting that subjectivity is constructed through an admixture of fluctuating material circumstances, embedded desires, creative memories, and habitual attachments. Subjectivity, according to this view, is never static; it is always in flux and is relationally constituted. On the other hand, an immaterialist would maintain that one's personal identity is immutable. The unchanging inner self is formed by properties, such as a timeless idea of "home," that functions as an a priori legislative image of thought, fixing a subject's identity in place. Identity here is defined negatively, through bipolar opposition: woman versus man, nature versus culture, and so on.

One way to philosophically deal with the aporetic conundrum that Albrecht's concept of solastalgia presents is to begin with the idea of a common world, which involves also infusing a transpeciesist logic into the concept, much as Indigenous cultures understand their connection to the earth and other animals. Indigenous communities share many tenets of Albrecht's existentialist view of human emotion and the psychological connection to home. The intimate connection and deep sense of belonging that Indigenous groups hold toward ancestral lands and waterways consistently reappears in Indigenous advocacy, in recognition of customary land and sea rights, in Indigenous cultural heritage and ancestral practices, and in biodiversity conservation. However, unlike the existentialist, Indigenous communities have a more collective view of habitat value. Habitat value, for the Indigenous Australians, as Marcia Langton has shown, is not easily quantified or clearly demarcated within the boundaries of an individual psyche or identity.[11]

The value that different Indigenous groups place on their environmental context is as much social and cultural as it is biophysical. Theirs is an expansive geosophical, relational, and animistic view of ecological relations. Indigenous communities embrace the sentience of other-than-human species. They hold a deep sensitivity for, and awareness of, a shared relatedness between other-than-human-animals and human-animals.[12] For instance, Australian Indigenous communities believe that other-than-human-animals are their ancestors, share a spirit with human-animals, and have a soul that human-animals can impart through cultural practices such as song or dance.[13]

It is at this relational threshold where the limits to individual independence lie and a more transpeciesist understanding of the animalia–habitat relation is awakened. An individual animal is always already ecological, is always already implicated in a complex tapestry of interdependencies, and is always already an open, albeit relatively stable and organized, structure that grows, is stimulated, and synthesizes energy.

Animalia–habitat relationships are instinctual, habitual, and inventive.[14] Instinctive attributes, behaviors, and skills, such as migration and herding, are innate, or, as the neuroscientist Mark Blumberg has described in relation to Charles Darwin's and Konrad Lorenz's understanding of instinct, such characteristics point to a "shared genetic heritage of widely divergent species" and can be defined as behavior that is "inborn, experience-independent, stereotypic, species-typical, inherited, learning-resistant, and unmodified by ongoing stimulation."[15] However, in the attempt to "explain the exquisite fit between organism and environment," Blumberg argues, the word *instinct* has come to refer to a "variety of complex behaviors."[16] Survival also depends upon reliably accessing shelter, locating water, and sourcing nutrition through the consumption of other organisms, all of which depend upon learning, repeating, and modifying certain behaviors. When the ecological reliability of a habitat is disturbed, degraded, diminished, fragmented, or lost completely, species must adapt or perish.[17]

Studies into species-typical behaviors show that instincts are not simply genetically determined. Rather, they emerge through a creative process of epigenesis that combines internal characteristics that are present at birth with external attributes learned through experience.[18] Ultimately, the boundary between the internal and external life of an animal is not hard-and-fast, nor is their relation hierarchically structured. Rather, the boundary is supple and porous. Their relationship to each other is complex, and neither an internal or external life is the "essential locus of control."[19] As Gilles Deleuze and Felix Guattari put it:

> We make no distinction between man and nature: the human essence of nature and the natural essence of man become one within nature in the form of production or industry, just as they do within the life of man as a species. Industry is then no longer considered from the extrinsic point of view of utility, but rather from the point of view of its fundamental identity with nature as production of man by man. Not man as the king of creation, but rather as the being who is in intimate contact with the profound life of all forms or all types of beings, who is responsible for even the stars and animal life, and who ceaselessly plugs an organ-machine into an energy-machine, a tree into his body, a breast into his mouth, the sun into his asshole.[20]

When we add into the mix random genetic mutation and the nonrandom process of natural selection that results in certain genetic mutations becoming more prevalent, the view that animalia autonomy indicates independence and self-sufficiency becomes murky. Recent scientific studies into animal instincts point to a more contextualized view of autonomy. In Blumberg's words:

> All complex behaviors are composed of sub-behaviors, each of which is induced at each stage of development, often in non-obvious ways. Thus DNA, cells, behavior, and our physical, social, and cultural environments interact continuously and dynamically, in real time, to create the behaviors that have revealed themselves to many as the products of divine or genetic design. Evolution, of course, plays a major role in the emergence of complex behavior, not by focusing its attention on genes, but by selecting for the entire developmental manifold.[21]

The autonomy of animalia (multicellular eukaryotic organisms) is complex. It includes a capacity for flexibility and an ability to respond creatively to new stimuli and circumstances. For instance, polar bears have reacted to declining sea ice by changing their diets—eating dolphins and snow goose eggs—and by moving ashore to forage on food that humans eat.[22] Autonomy, however, is impacted by the rate at which a context changes. In the case of polar bears, Arctic climatic conditions are changing much faster than the bear can effectively respond. As such, although all bears (*ursids*) "show behavioural plasticity," given "the rapid pace of ecological change in the Arctic, the long generation time, and the highly specialised nature of polar bears, it is unlikely that polar bears will survive as a species if the sea ice disappears completely."[23]

Now we come full circle, returning to that three-year-old white polar bear cub condemned to a life of perpetual display inside a mall in China. The sadness of the saddest polar bear in the world is as much about an animality lost for all time as it is about the inhumanity gripping *Homo sapiens* animality. Each represents a heightened experience of estrangement and events of acute vanishing. The sadness animal rights activists detect, then, is as much their own as it is the bear cub's. It is an inhumane weight that humanity currently shoulders as it persistently pushes the majority of life on earth, including itself, toward extinction.[24]

The symbols wrested forth from the alienation of this lone bear cub—of other-than-human-animal suffering and of the fraught relationship between other-than-human-animals and human-animals—were so powerful in their affective reach that they traversed all manner of differences distinguishing one person from the next, stopping a collective imagination dead in its tracks. The distressed images of one lone species reverberated far and wide, and in so doing, the images served as an evocative reminder of the many lives that the human species has forced to the brink of annihilation. In this light, the sadness animal advocacy groups spoke of is as much a sadness arising from the incalculable disappearance of all things great and small as it is a sadness that comes from the realization that vast sections of humanity are bereft of their humanity, devoid of the very conditions that are the building blocks of human existence. How else to explain the jubilant excitement of mall patrons posing alongside another earthling's suffering, images of which they then flippantly share via Instagram postings and Snapchat snaps?

In all the frames taken of Pizza and disseminated through social and mainstream media, the cub is unquestionably tormented. The violence inherent to the speed of such a self-absorbed instant comes from the manner in which the snapshot legitimates the user's power by invalidating the gravity of the animal's afflicted state.[25] An autobiographical imaging that is taken at the expense of another living being's suffering is not an expression of autonomy; it is an abuse of power that can occur under circumstances of empathic numbness. It is an image that conjures up a sadness in the viewer, who is concomitantly turned into the witness of a terrible atrocity, an image that institutes a frame of human experience and understanding by invoking the double-edged sword of animality. Here, the otherness of the other-than-human animal is the dark underbelly of human animality that the human performs and thinks through.

In the technological apparatus of framing, imaging, and image dissemination, a field of power relations is established, whereby the power differential between human-animals and the other-than-human animal institutes multiple instances of human authority and agency—image production, distribution, and consumption. And let's not forget the facility owners, animal trainers, and even animal rights advocates who participate in the mechanics of desiring-production that the selfies set in motion. The very act of imaging the captive other-than-human animal, then subjecting it both to the gaze of the onlooker in the mall and later to the viewer witnessing the act, establishes a double mediation and objectification.

"Essential here is the necessary interplay between subjectivism and objectivism," as Martin Heidegger once noted, such that the human "becomes the primary and only *real subjectum* . . . the relational center of that which is as such." To continue with Heidegger on this point, "This objectifying of whatever is, is accomplished in a setting-before, a representing that aims at bringing each particular being before it in such a way that man who calculates can be sure, and that means be certain of that being." Put differently, the other-than-human-animal comes into existence in mediated form, once as representation and second as human spectacle, instituting the human-as-agent, "the being upon which all that is, is grounded."[26] That grounding comes at the expense of the other-than-human-animal. It is the result of a misplaced use and abuse of power that frames, tames, and claims the wildness of the other-than-human-animal as the property of the human, and the tool through which humanity recognizes itself.

What if the display glass erasing "the long human history of the exploitation and despoliation of aquatic environments," as Ian

Buchanan describes the screened-off microcosmic worlds aquariums present, were removed?[27] Then the other-than-human animal would no longer appear behind the human-animal; it would stand alongside or in front of it, the shift in positionality marking an ontological shift in point of view, as Jacques Derrida astutely points out in *The Animal That Therefore I Am*. At issue here are the "the *unprecedented* proportions of this subjection of the animal" by human-animals.[28] Speaking on the images of animal abuse that proliferate throughout culture, Derrida explains:

> If these images are "pathetic," if they evoke sympathy, it is also because they "pathetically" open the immense question of pathos and the pathological, precisely, that is, of suffering, pity, and compassion: and the place that has to be accorded to the interpretation of this compassion, to the sharing of this suffering among the living, to the law, ethics, and politics that must be brought to bear upon this experience of compassion.[29]

The selfies with Pizza neatly encapsulate the inhumanity of humanity, when humanity is bereft of compassion and reciprocity. It is the staging of another animal's erasure as the site of human recognition, assertion, and self-determination.[30] Understood this way, the Pizza selfies invoke an age-old indissoluble boundary between human-animals and other-than-human animals. For Derrida, this speciesist division harks all the way back to the opening pages of the Old Testament, when "God gives Ish alone the freedom to name the animals, granted, and that represents at the same time his sovereignty and his loneliness."[31] The boundary between human-animals and other-than-human-animals institutes a false claim to ontological difference and privilege in the kingdom of animalia.

What if the body of this human-animal had unexpectedly stumbled naked upon the other-than-human animal? Had the polar bear cub observed a bare human-animal, encountering it "*frontally* naked," in the way that Derrida once playfully speculated, then maybe a sense of self-reflexive shame would have set in for the human-animal. Unclothed, and "naked as a beast," the human-animal may have instead admitted to "being ashamed of being ashamed" and a shared animality may have ignited there.[32]

Had the displays, cameras, and clothing screens been eliminated, maybe then the "animal could *look* at them, and *address* them . . . from a wholly other origin," from a position that no longer placed it in the service of human-animal well-being.[33] As the other-than-human animal's eyes stare, glare, peruse, and scrutinize the undisguised human-animal body, a human-beast is exposed. Standing disrobed before the other-than-human animal, the egregious indifference the human-animal showed to the other may have been challenged.

Stripped bare of T-shirts, jeans, underwear, socks, and shoes, the substantive verification of a shared animality would have been uncloaked and exposed. After all, *Homo sapiens* shares 98.7% of their DNA with chimpanzees (*Pan troglodytes*) and bonobos (*Pan paniscus*).[34] Perhaps under these circumstances the power dynamic of a selfie moment taken in the Grandview shopping mall would have been defused in a collective moment of animality, disarming the endless stampede of spectators of their manufactured anthropocentric advantage. That advantage is not innate; it is a constructed, speciesist social structure that, as Derrida noted, has reduced "the animal not only to production and overactive reproduction" but also to "meat for human consumption" and "all sorts of other end products," an abstract difference invoked by human-animals to mask the concrete reality that they are engaging in the mass murder of their ancestors.[35]

TABLE 7.1
Species Conservation Status

Common Name	Scientific Name	Conservation Status
Amur leopard	*Panthera pardus orientalis*	Critically endangered
Black rhino	*Diceros bicornis*	Critically endangered
Bornean orangutan	*Pongo pygmaeus*	Critically endangered
Cross river gorilla	*Gorilla gorilla diehli*	Critically endangered
Eastern lowland gorilla	*Gorilla beringei graueri*	Critically endangered
Hawksbill turtle	*Eretmochelys imbricata*	Critically endangered
Javan rhino	*Rhinoceros sondaicus*	Critically endangered
Orangutan	*Pongo abelii, Pongo pygmaeus*	Critically endangered
Saola	*Pseudoryx nghetinhensis*	Critically endangered
Sumatran elephant	*Elephas maximus sumatranus*	Critically endangered
Sumatran orangutan	*Pongo abelii*	Critically endangered
Sumatran rhino	*Dicerorhinus sumatrensis*	Critically endangered
Sunda tiger	*Panthera tigris sondaica*	Critically endangered
Vaquita	*Phocoena sinus*	Critically endangered
Western lowland gorilla	*Gorilla gorilla gorilla*	Critically endangered
Yangtze finless porpoise	*Neophocaena asiaeorientalis ssp. asiaeorientalis*	Critically endangered
African wild dog	*Lycaon pictus*	Endangered
Asian elephant	*Elephas maximus indicus*	Endangered
Black-footed ferret	*Mustela nigripes*	Endangered
Blue whale	*Balaenoptera musculus*	Endangered
Bluefin tuna	*Thunnus thynnus*	Endangered
Bonobo	*Pan paniscus*	Endangered
Bornean elephant	*Elephas maximus borneensis*	Endangered
Chimpanzee	*Pan troglodytes*	Endangered
Fin whale	*Balaenoptera physalus*	Endangered
Galápagos penguin	*Spheniscus mendiculus*	Endangered
Ganges river dolphin	*Platanista gangetica gangetica*	Endangered
Green turtle	*Chelonia mydas*	Endangered
Hector's dolphin	*Cephalorhynchus hectori*	Endangered
Humphead wrasse	*Cheilinus undulatus*	Endangered
Indian elephant	*Elephas maximus indicus*	Endangered
Indus River dolphin	*Platanista minor*	Endangered
Irrawaddy dolphin	*Orcaella brevirostris*	Endangered
Mountain gorilla	*Gorilla beringei beringei*	Endangered

(continued)

TABLE 7.1 (continued)

Common Name	Scientific Name	Conservation Status
North Atlantic right whale	*Eubalaena glacialis*	Endangered
Red panda	*Ailurus fulgens*	Endangered
Sea lions	*Zalophus wollebaeki*	Endangered
Sea turtle	*Cheloniidae* and *Dermochelyidae* families	Endangered
Sei whale	*Balaenoptera borealis*	Endangered
Sri Lankan elephant	*Elephas maximus maximus*	Endangered
Tiger	*Panthera tigris*	Endangered
Whale	*Balaenoptera, Balaena, Eschrichtius,* and *Eubalaen*	Endangered
Whale shark	*Rhincodon typus*	Endangered
African elephant	*Loxodonta africana*	Vulnerable
Bigeye tuna	*Thunnus obesus*	Vulnerable
Black spider monkey	*Ateles paniscus*	Vulnerable
Dugong	*Dugong dugon*	Vulnerable
Forest elephant	—	Vulnerable
Giant panda	*Ailuropoda melanoleuca*	Vulnerable
Giant tortoise	—	Vulnerable
Great white shark	*Carcharodan carcharias*	Vulnerable
Greater one-horned rhino	*Rhinoceros unicornis*	Vulnerable
Hippopotamus	*Hippopotamus amphibius*	Vulnerable
Leatherback turtle	*Dermochelys coriacea*	Vulnerable
Marine iguana	*Amblyrhynchus cristatus*	Vulnerable
Olive ridley turtle	*Lepidochelys olivacea*	Vulnerable
Polar bear	*Ursus maritimus*	Vulnerable
Savanna elephant	*Loxodonta africana africana*	Vulnerable
Snow leopard	*Panthera uncia*	Vulnerable
Southern rockhopper penguin	*Eudyptes chrysocome*	Vulnerable
Albacore tuna	*Thunnus alalunga*	Near threatened
Beluga	*Delphinapterus leucas*	Near threatened
Greater sage-grouse	*Centrocercus urophasianus*	Near threatened
Jaguar	*Panthera onca*	Near threatened
Mountain plover	*Charadrius montanus*	Near threatened
Narwhal	*Monodon monoceros*	Near threatened
Plains bison	*Bison bison bison*	Near threatened
White rhino	*Ceratotherium simum*	Near threatened
Yellowfin tuna	*Thunnus albacares*	Near threatened

Source: World Wildlife Fund, "Species Directory," https://www.worldwildlife.org/species/directory?direction=desc&sort=extinction_status. Accessed October 11, 2021.

{ 8 }

Eco-ontology

AND THERE I WAS, WAITING, inside the lion's den of one of the world's biggest oil moguls. I had been granted a one-hour time slot to briefly cover introductions before moving on to what was really up for grabs: an impoverished rural town in a godforsaken part of the country. He hoped I would advise him on how to best drill the heck out of every last inch of solace that place provided for a few thousand people who called it home, while also enabling him to make a swift, clean exit, with his reputation intact, when the wells eventually ran dry.

The well-meaning community development director in the corner of the office smiled eagerly and spoke up only when spoken to. I looked wistfully out the glass windows, which extended the full height of the room, onto the corporate-backed horizon line of Big D, wondering how much longer all of this would take. The mogul assertively leaned back. His wide, polished grin was adorned with two neatly packed rows of $100,000 pearly whites. He beamed roguishly my way.

"Can't believe I'm here with Adrian Parr, the environmentalist!" he boomed.

"Can't believe I'm here with a fossil fuel magnate," I sardonically responded.

He rocked impatiently in his oversize black leather chair, nonchalantly clasping his immaculately manicured hands behind his head. His eyes cheekily snapped mine to attention. A few seconds later, he dumped his long, heavy legs onto the desk between us. His Lucchese ostrich cowboy boots pointed straight up at me, daring me to comment. I didn't take the bait. My eyes quietly held his gaze.

The conundrum he faced: How could he put a spin on the environmental and social wreckage he would create and still be viewed as the generous philanthropist he had convinced himself he was? Of course, the concern in question was not so weighty that it kept him up at night. It was more like an irritable itch than an agonizing anxiety, but it was an aggravation nonetheless.

So here I was, poised for the big ask: Could I advise on how he might do all this . . . sustainably?

That set the tone for what became a prolonged sparring match.

We ran around and around in circles. The time had come to cut him short, to stop wasting my time and make a concrete choice to remove myself from this ecologically illiterate and vicious circle of economically motivated ethical blight.

> I refuse to be your bottom girl on lease,
> managing your risks to keep the peace,
> as you drill baby drill,
> never looking back
> at the ugly fact
> that you are a pimp,
> seducing piss-poor communities
> with brief flings at job security,
> prostituting land for short-term gain
> and all that bling
> that comes from narcissistic insanity.
> You, sir,
> are in the business of committing crimes
> against humanity.
> The best thing you can do
> is not blur
> the line between
> myth and reality.
> Let their home be,
> and shift to clean energy.

I could hear him roar with laughter from behind closed doors, shouting that we weren't finished yet. Indeed, he was right, but not in the way he intended.

If humanity continues destroying the world's ecosystems, pumping greenhouse gases into the atmosphere, consuming the earth's resources faster than the earth can replenish them, poisoning and draining freshwater reserves, engaging in the mass murder of other-than-human species, the question will not be how to survive but rather what form survival will take. The countdown is on: either *Homo sapiens* makes a choice to shift course or the earth will make it for us. If the warnings issued by the scientific and academic communities are any indication, survival may very well be a considerably compromised life teetering at the ecological limits of existence. The immanent life emanating out of the ecocidal remains of anthropocentric history is potentially a life pillaged of enriching complexity and wonder. In her study of mass extinctions dating back nearly 500 million years, Elizabeth Kolbert reaffirms the view that human activities in the age of the Anthropocene not only categorically threaten other-than-human life but also threaten the very basis of human life itself. Quoting biologist Paul Ehrlich, she states, "In pushing other species to extinction, humanity is busy sawing off the limb on which it perches."[1]

In 2018, forty-two scientists from around the world published a study on the terrestrial impact of climate science. In order to better understand and predict terrestrial ecological changes under current and future climate scenarios, the team studied fossil records dating back to the last period of deglaciation on earth, approximately 21,000 years ago. This was a time when the earth underwent 4°C to 7°C of warming, and it serves as a useful scientific benchmark to study how vegetation responds to a warming climate. Existing climate warming scenarios warn of anywhere up to 5°C of warming above preindustrial levels by the end of this century, if we continue with business as usual. This review of 594 paleoecological records showed that "terrestrial ecosystems are highly sensitive to temperature change," and the findings also "suggest that without major reductions in greenhouse gas emissions to the atmosphere, terrestrial ecosystems worldwide are at risk of major transformation, with accompanying disruption of ecosystem services and impacts on biodiversity."[2] Furthermore, the primary difference between the two periods of climate warming, then and now, is that the previous period of deglaciation occurred over a span of 10,000 to 20,000 years. Present-day climate warming, by contrast, is taking place over a few centuries, thereby compromising species adaptation and the integrity of biophysical systems. The authors concluded that at this rate, human beings, who are terrestrial creatures, have a bleak albeit temporary future ahead of them.

Similarly, a 2019 report from the Intergovernmental Science-Policy Platform on Biodiversity and Ecosystem Services (IPBES) warns that over the next few decades the earth could lose nearly a million plant and animal species. Human extraction of resources and waste production alone have dramatically altered the world's climate system, intact ecosystems, the productivity of the land, and more. The IPBES states that human activities have "significantly altered" 75% of terrestrial environments and 66% of marine environments. Approximately "60 billion tons of renewable and nonrenewable resources" are extracted annually—double what it was in 1980.[3] Over the past two centuries, approximately one-third of global forest cover has disappeared.

Put succinctly, human actions are decimating the living world, and for what? As I and others, such as Naomi Klein, John Bellamy Foster, Brett Clark, Richard York, and George Monbiot, to name a few, have consistently argued, this situation is structural. The obdurate global economic system of capital accumulation has locked all life on earth into ecological collapse.[4] That said, capitalism is a choice. A different path could be chosen and created.

The silver lining of the 2020 global COVID-19 pandemic is that it lent credence to the idea and reality that alternative socioeconomic modalities are possible. Writing during the pandemic and in response to the shutdown, Bruno Latour made a timely and heartfelt plea: "It is right now that we have to fight so that the economic recovery, once the crisis has passed, does not bring back the same former climatic regime against which we were battling, until now somewhat in vain."[5]

COVID-19 brought about a massive change in human behavior as people were forced to physically distance. The changes were so remarkable that they could be seen from space. At the fall American Geophysical Union meeting held on December 7, 2020, scientists studying satellite images and Landsat data compared environmental conditions before and during COVID-19. They reported, "Deforestation rates are changing in some places, air pollution is diminishing, water quality is improving, and snow is becoming more reflective in some areas since the pandemic began earlier this year."[6] The freeways had come to a grinding halt, industrial activities were slowed if not stopped entirely, streets quieted, pedestrian activity took over, wildlife was heard again in urban areas, greenhouse gas emissions were set on pause, and the earth's skies cleared of smog and pollutants.

The sudden and remarkable environmental bounce-back that occurred during the pandemic prompted Latour to draw attention to a few key take-home lessons:

> The first lesson the coronavirus has taught us is also the most astounding: we have actually proven that it is possible, in a few weeks, to put an economic system on hold everywhere in the world and at the same time, a system that we were told it was impossible to slow down or redirect. To every ecologist's argument about changing our ways of life, there was always the opposing argument about the irreversible force of the "train of progress" that nothing could derail "because of globalisation," they would say. And yet it is precisely its globalised character that makes this infamous development so fragile, so likely to do the opposite and come to a screeching halt....
>
> Now is the time for the annual stock-take. When common sense asks us to "start production up again as quickly as

possible," we have to shout back, "Absolutely not!" The last thing to do is repeat the exact same thing we were doing before.[7]

The "exact same thing" Latour refers to is inexorable consumption and global economic growth, to the point where even the greening of economic growth, as I have argued previously, is a violent misnomer and dangerous displacement activity.[8]

As human activities transition the great earth system that James Lovelock calls Gaia into a "hot and inhospitable state," the temporality of human history is disrupting and devastating the qualitative timelessness of the earth system.[9] The physical spaces of ruination that species and ecosystems increasingly inhabit are fast becoming the repositories of a collective traumatic experience, subjecting all living entities to perpetual ecocide. Lawyer and environmental activist Polly Higgins was deeply committed to bringing international recognition to the illegality of ecocide. She likened the far-reaching destruction ecocide inflicts to that of waging war, dedicating her entire professional life to advancing peace by means of advocating for the introduction of international laws designed to "prevent, pre-empt, and prohibit" crimes of ecocide. Ecocide, she explains, denotes "*the extensive destruction, damage to or loss of ecosystem(s) of a given territory, whether by human agency or by other causes, to such an extent that peaceful enjoyment by the inhabitants of that territory has been severely diminished.*"[10]

The transnational character of both how ecocide comes about and the destructive impact of ecocidal acts demands a collective response and systems of accountability that extend beyond the borders of sovereign states. This begins with crafting a legal language that can be used both to outlaw ecocide and for principles of governance. Higgins formed a categorical distinction between non-ascertainable and ascertainable ecocide. An example of the former, she maintained, is a destructive loss to a territory without liability, whereas the latter is an instance in which criminal liability can be determined based on three measurable categories of criminality: destruction, loss, and damage.

Drawing on language developed by the United Nations and incorporated into international laws of warfare, Higgins proposed the following conceptual framework to articulate how ecocide functions as a crime against peace. First, the effects of destructive actions are spatial; they can be measured according to the impact wrought over a particular area. Second, loss is a durational category; it is ascertained by how long-lasting the harm is. Third, damage is a qualitative intensity that is gauged according to the severity and quality of injury perpetrated against a specific life form. To this day, the legal value of ecosystems as premised upon a theory of peace continues to gain traction.

In her recent work on the force of nonviolence, Judith Butler points out that radical equality emerges when no one life is valued more than another.[11] She explains that at the heart of the problem of nonviolence is the inherent relationality, or sociality, of the self. The current state of ecological affairs points to a critical void in how human beings understand not only what they value but also their own value. Following Butler's logic on violence, we find that because our lives do not take place in a vacuum, when we inflict violence on another being we are in effect harming ourselves. According to this reasoning, harming the earth's life support system for millions of plant and animal species inevitably harms us. Every act of violence, whether systemic, institutional, individual, or otherwise, involves a value proposition that demarcates one life as more valuable than another.

In his extensive work on violence, theorist Brad Evans warns against formulating conceptions of the political around endangerment, arguing that this ensnares our understanding and practice of politics within a narrative of security.[12] Evans rightly cautions that this has implications for how human beings organize and relate to one another. Namely, the presupposition of endangerment produces a defensively structured social organization. I would agree with Evans, and for this reason the ecological principle of mutual flourishing must push out in front of the widely circulating narrative of impending doom.

Placing collective well-being ahead of the overarching narratives of resilience and security is not to be mistaken for holding the gravity of the ecological situation in contempt, nor is it intended to undermine the validity of climate and environmental science. On the contrary, trust in the science calls for a complete overhaul of what is valued and how. The idea that the future poses a perilous existence is in itself a political position. It is ideological in that it argues for a specific version of the future, accordingly closing it off from its very own futurity, from the possibility of the future being different from what currently is. All conceptions of the future are inevitably political because they concern different ways in which the future is used, which ultimately aligns with different kinds of value. Hence, invoking a future of mutual flourishing as a lens through which political discourses and practices work necessarily means moving toward a future in which deep democracy has taken hold and global capitalism has been left behind, a vestige of a dark turn in human history.

The principle of mutual flourishing doesn't negate individual agency and freedoms; it merely proposes that such freedoms can never be at the expense of another—otherwise, it is no longer freedom that is at work but oppression and exploitation. It recognizes that transnational justice, transgenerational fairness, and transspeciesist existence are today's contemporary sites of political struggle. Helping such a transenvironmental framework gain traction, though, is no easy feat, if the recent turn toward right-wing populist politics is any indication.

Henry Giroux brilliantly argues that left-wing politics has sold itself short in its focus on the economic realm as the primary locus of political change. Giroux underscores the importance of critical pedagogy in overcoming civic illiteracy and what he calls the "dead zones of imagination," by teaching students how to think critically.[13] Education is crucial to nurturing an engaged and informed citizenry capable of and willing to stand up against the violence extreme right-wing groups pose. The new turn to the far right at the beginning of the twenty-first century is mobilized by hatred, alternative facts, and shared anxieties. This is a politics that confirms its authority through tactics of intimidation and fear and mockingly turns its back on empathy, compassion, and an ecological conscience. Santiago Zabala chillingly reminds us of the stakes: the greatest emergencies are the ones not faced.[14]

Over the past few hundred years a variety of mechanisms and institutions have been developed to expand and support the range of what society values and how value is safeguarded. Policies and legislation, such as the recent call to institute an international law against ecocide, enable us to take responsibility for what society deems valuable. In addition, there is a growing global movement pushing the language of rights beyond that of mere property relations, calling for legal frameworks that recognize the relational and enriching value that ecosystems hold for the flourishing of all life on earth. In 2017, New Zealand and India granted rights to important waterways. The Whanganui River in New Zealand was the first river to be granted legal personhood status. Five days later, India followed suit, granting the Ganges and Yamuna Rivers legal rights.[15]

Constitutions and treaties also can be used to collectively decide what people value. In 2008, Ecuador bravely led the way in incorporating the rights of the earth into its constitution. Then, in 2009, the people of Bolivia voted in a new constitution that recognized the collective value of the environment. At a United Nations press conference held on January 27, 2009, the Bolivian deputy permanent representative to the United Nations, Pablo Solón-Romero, explained that the new Indigenous- and earth-friendly constitutional text would prevent "the recurrence of any processes of privatization of State corporations and natural resources" as well as increase the rights of "all Bolivians, especially indigenous people and other groups."[16]

The holophytic system of the planet has neither exteriority nor a unified internal mechanism whereby the death of a part would necessarily mean the demise of the whole. That said, the viability of each and every life form on earth relies upon the recycling motion of Gaia as it generates its own energy, synthesizing inorganic substances through the use of sunlight. The ecological overreach resulting from human activities demands a deepening of humanity and a radical reimagining of humanity as ecological. The challenge we collectively face is to transcend the human–environment dichotomy that, despite all good intentions, anthropocentrically frames environmental laws and policies, sustainability culture, green governance, and the greening of the free market.

If, as Lovelock argues, Gaia is a complex and indivisible earth system, then it also holds that humans are a micro-ecological process embedded within varying ecological scales and time frames and are altogether implicated in the larger ecological earth process known as Gaia. The concept of the Anthropocene (*anthro* meaning "human," *cene* meaning "new") points to a new human-induced geological epoch in the history of the earth, but this does not mean that human concerns inevitably override or are prior to ecological ones. As the human worldview gradually wakes up to fact that all life forms are part of a super motion of planetary being— Gaia—the realization that humanity can only ever be conditionally constituted takes hold, for humanity is muted, if not vacated entirely, in the absence of ecological well-being.

If we continue on this path, it is game over for the majority of life on earth as we know it. As such, the questions humanity poses moving forward, as it sets out to engage human agency and bring about transformative change in response to the mounting gravity ecological ruination presents for all life on earth, must commence with an eco-ontological framework. Such a framework must effectively unravel the anthropocentric norms that have shaped human exceptionalism and have been used to justify the concomitant ruination of the earth's climate, the loss of species and biodiversity, the collapse of ecosystems, and the violence this unleashes upon marginalized communities.

If, as I have argued elsewhere, we urgently need to be activating an emancipatory and inclusive imagination, then by its very definition this would mean an imagination premised upon the flourishing of all life, both today and in the future.[17] This is nothing short of galvanizing an eco-ontological weltanschauung, a collectivist activism that moves beyond the anthropocentric framing of humanism and identity politics that Rosi Braidotti has so astutely underscored in her work.[18] The challenge is to recognize that all life on earth is ecological, which means that reciprocity, not outdated notions of identity and individuality, must become the driving force of politics and social life.

The emancipatory inclusive imagination I outlined in *Birth of a New Earth* invoked the force of utopian thinking to argue for a nonidealistic approach to the imagination, one that is put to work to articulate an aspirational reality. The transformative power of the imagination lies in three areas. First, the imagination is both an individual and a collective faculty of affect; it has the capacity to pry open new corporeal spaces of feeling and emotion. Second, it is strategic; it can be used to access the unknown and stretch the horizon of what is actual by massaging the undiscovered potential latent within actually existing circumstances. Third, it is a cultural apparatus that amplifies, disseminates, and validates value; it can be invoked as a site of criticality or repression.

In short, there is a politics to how notions of reality are articulated and used, as these circumscribe the limits of what is both possible and imaginable. Whether we are speaking of the radical equality Butler invokes, the Gaia hypothesis of James Lovelock and Lynn Margulis, the political ecology Latour expounds, the relationality Braidotti invokes, or the politics of commoning and the role an emancipatory imagination plays in realizing this, to which I have appealed, we are all emphasizing in our respective ways one simple idea: a singular life does not exist in a vacuum; it is intrinsically structured and sustained through myriad interdependencies.[19]

{ 9 }

Re-commencement

SCIENCE TEACHES US the earth is approximately
    4.5 billion years old.
Today the average lifetime of a person living in
    the U.S. is 78.
That means each and every one of our lives is barely a
    second's worth of the earth's lifetime.

We are all but a snap of the finger in earth time.
What will you choose to do with your flash of a second?

Will it be a wide-eyed vibe,
All fearless and spunk?
Flooding generosity,
and sensitivity
into a world
that till 200,000 years ago
lived vacant of human history?

Perhaps your second
will be the power
of a beaming smile
seducing naysayers and the hostile,
turning the impossible, possible,
making compassion
and conscience credible.

A second,
celebrating those who dare rise
in a flash of audacity,
from the stigmas and stereotypes
defining,
and inscribing,
love's infinite capacity.

RE-COMMENCEMENT

Maybe that second you get,
is a simple footstep,
resolutely re-directing
narrow mindedness,
bigotry,
and hatred.

Sometimes all it takes
is the steadfast stride of humanity
flooding the landfills of inequity,
extinguishing the animosity
circumscribing human difference as absolute
and beyond refute.

Or, it's a bite of your lip,
that second
you encounter life's trivialities,
followed by a defiant shout
out
against misplaced legalities
betraying forever rising seas,
and thousands of vanishing species.

If, in that second
living narrows and knots,
you feel you can't cope,
take pause,
hang up the oars,
let that lifeboat silently float,
watch the clouds vaguely swell and unravel.
Wait it out till the many forevers reappear,
cause they always
eventually do

as the fog settles and surrenders
to lighter spheres.

Who are we?
We are the many clicks,
blinks,
winks,
sighs,
and smiles
that together create history.

We are each and every one of us
a mere second of earthly consent
amongst the vastness
Four and a half billion earth years presents.

A single generation
amidst the tick tock
of several more
and countless befores.

So don't be stuck in your second
without mystery,
with unconfirmed shadows
and untold secrets
of some 5,000 years of recorded human history.

A second,
a wink,
a flash,
and a snap!

Go,
put your compassion to work.

RE-COMMENCEMENT

Make your second of this earth's life matter.
Respond unequivocally,
Unflinchingly,
with feverish integrity
to the miraculous,
the marvelous,
the ruined and wrecked.

Be a thunderclap
to a drought-filled field;
a proud blue glacier
brightening the souls of us all.
Be happy for hope unconcealed,
and the joy others feel.

Be guided by the kindness you give
not the things you buy,
nor the objects you own,
but the lives
you enrich,
the hope
you build,
the curiosity
you help grow.
That's where riches lie
and where unpretentious
futures are sown.

Be of this time,
Not a relic from another.
Find your relevance,
your very own punch line.

Now it's your time
to brighten the world,

to glide and soar
with wit and wonder;
to become the very best version of *you*.

'Cause all it takes is a second,
a wink,
a flash,
and a snap
of earthtime
to be a breakthrough
for tomorrow to continue.

And that's a wrap.

Notes

Commencement

1. See James Lovelock, *The Revenge of Gaia: Earth's Climate Crisis and the Fate of Humanity* (New York: Basic Books, 2007); and Bill McKibben, *Earth: Making a Life on a Tough New Planet* (New York: Henry Holt, 2010).
2. Ideas for the development of a trans-environmentalism first appeared in a short essay published in 2019, and then later in 2020 as part of an interview I gave. See Adrian Parr, "The Great Slumber... and Then There Were None," in *Los Angeles Review of Books*, September 9, 2019; Margarita Jover Biboum, Rubén García Rubio, and Carlos Ávila Calzada, "Adrian Parr, a Polyhedral Relationship with Water," *ZARCH* 15 (December 2020): 188–195.
3. Karen Barad, *Meeting the Universe Halfway: Quantum Physics and the Entanglement of Matter and Meaning* (Durham, NC: Duke University Press, 2007), 26.
4. Madeline Weiss et al., "The Physiology and Habitat of the Last Universal Common Ancestor," *Nature Microbiology* 1, no. 9 (July 2016): 16116.
5. Traci Watson, "The Trickster Microbes That Are Shaking Up the Tree of Life," *Nature* 569 (May 2019): 322–324.

1. Land

1. James Lovelock, *Gaia: A New Look at Life on Earth*, 3rd rev. ed. (Oxford: Oxford University Press, 2000).

2. Stephen Scully, *Hesiod's Theogony: From Near Eastern Creation Myths to Paradise Lost* (Oxford: Oxford University Press, 2015).

3. Peter Ward, *The Medea Hypothesis: Is Life on Earth Ultimately Self-Destructive?* (Princeton, NJ: Princeton University Press, 2009).

4. Anthony Cilluffo and Neil G. Ruiz, "World's Population Is Projected to Nearly Stop Growing by the End of the Century," Pew Research Center, June 17, 2019.

5. Edward O. Wilson, *The Future of Life* (New York: Knopf, 2002).

6. Michael Hendryx and Mellisa Ahern, "Mortality in Appalachian Coal Mining Regions: The Value of Statistical Life Lost," *Public Health Reports* 124, no. 4 (July–August 2009): 541–550; Leigh-Anne Krometis et al., "Environmental Health Disparities in the Central Appalachian Region of the United States," *Reviews on Environmental Health* 32, no. 3 (September 2017): 253–266.

7. Appalachian Regional Commission, "ARC Announces $3.3 Million to Continue Economic Growth in Region's Coal-Impacted Communities," February 12, 2020.

8. Patrick Canning et al., *The Role of Fossil Fuels in the U.S. Food System and the American Diet*, United States Department of Agriculture, Economic Research Report no. 224 (January 2017): 42.

9. United Nations Forum on Forests, *United Nations Strategic Plan for Forests 2030*, briefing note.

10. Charles Coble, Elaine Murray, and Dole Rice, *Earth Science* (Englewood Cliffs, NJ: Prentice-Hall, 1987), 102; Food and Agricultural Organization of the United Nations, *Global Forest Resources Assessment 2010*, FAO Forestry Paper 163 (Rome: FAO, 2010), xiii.

11. David Gibbs, Nancy Harris, and Frances Seymour, "By the Numbers: The Value of Tropical Forests in the Climate Change Equation," World Resources Institute, October 4, 2018.

12. Rasmussen, Carol, "NASA Finds Good News on Forests and Carbon Dioxide," National Aeronautics and Space Administration, December 29, 2014.

13. Benjamin Gaubert et al., "Global Atmospheric CO_2 Inverse Models Converging on Neutral Tropical Land Exchange, but Disagreeing on Fossil Fuel and Atmospheric Growth Rate," *Biogeosciences* 16 (2019): 117–134.

14. Amazon Watch, "Another Amazonian Indigenous Leader Is Murdered in Brazil," press release, March 31, 2020.

15. Data was collected by the National Institute for Space Research (INPE), using satellite images. Monica de Bolle, *The Amazon Is a Carbon Bomb: How Can Brazil and the World Work Together to Avoid Setting It Off?*

(Washington, DC: Peterson Institute for International Economics, November 1, 2019), 3.

16. Heather Pringle, "In Peril," *Science* 348, no. 6239 (June 2015): 1080–1085.

17. Efigenia de Melo, Carlos Alberto Cid Ferreira, and Rogerio Gribel, "A New Species of *Coccoloba* P. Browne (Polygonaceae) from the Brazilian Amazon with Exceptionally Large Leaves," *Acta Amazonica* 49, no. 4 (2019): 324–329.

18. World Wildlife Fund, "Inside the Amazon," https://wwf.panda.org/knowl edge_hub/where_we_work/amazon/about_the_amazon.

19. Anne E. Barkley et al., "African Biomass Burning Is a Substantial Source of Phosphorus Deposition to the Amazon, Tropical Atlantic Ocean, and Southern Ocean," *Proceedings of the National Academy of Sciences* 116, no. 33 (August 2019): 16216–16221.

20. Robyn Burnham and Kirk Johnson, "South American Palaeobotany and the Origins of Neotropical Rainforests," *Philosophical Transactions of the Royal Society* 359, no. 1450 (October 29, 2004): 1595–1610.

21. Hans ter Steege et al., "Hyperdominance in the Amazonian Tree Flora," *Science* 342, no. 6156 (October 2013): 1243092.

22. Sophie Fauset et al., "Hyperdominance in Amazonian Forest Carbon Recycling," *Nature Communications* 6, article no. 6857 (April 2015).

23. United Nations Environment Programme, "Evaluate Land to Halt Annual Loss of 24 Billion Tonnes of Fertile Soil, Expert Panel Says," press release, June 17, 2016.

24. National Aeronautics and Space Administration, Goddard Institute for Space Studies, "GISS Surface Temperature Analysis."

2. Parasite

I use the definition of a parasite devised by Benny Borremans and his research team: "All organisms that infect, and are transmitted between, hosts. This includes pathogenic as well as non-pathogenic microparasites and macroparasites. This encompasses a wide range of characteristics." Benny Borremans et al., "Cross-Species Pathogen Spillover Across Ecosystem Boundaries: Mechanisms and Theory," *Philosophical Transactions of the Royal Society London B: Biological Sciences* 374, no. 1782 (September 2019): 20180344.

1. Helene Hiwat and Gustavo Bretas, "Ecology of *Anopheles darlingi* Root with Respect to Vector Importance: A Review," *Parasites and Vectors* 4, no. 1 (September 2011).

2. U.S. Centers for Disease Control and Prevention, "Malaria: Biology," July 16, 2020.

3. Scott Westenberger et al., "A Systems-Based Analysis of *Plasmodium vivax* Lifecycle Transcription from Human to Mosquito," *PLOS Neglected Tropical Diseases* 4, no. 4 (April 2010): e653.

4. S. G. Welch, I. A. McGregor, and K. Williams "The Duffy Blood Group and Malaria Prevalence in Gambian West Africa," *Transactions of the Royal Society of Tropical Medicine and Hygiene* 71, no. 4 (January 1977): 295–296.

5. Joseli Oliveira-Ferreira et al., "Malaria in Brazil: An Overview," *Malaria Journal* 9, no. 115 (April 30, 2010).

6. Bianca Carlos et al., "A Comprehensive Analysis of Malaria Transmission in Brazil," *Pathogens and Global Health* 113, no. 1 (February 2019): 1–13.

7. Andrew MacDonald and Erin Mordecai, "Amazon Deforestation Drives Malaria Transmission, and Malaria Burden Reduces Forest Clearing," *Proceedings of the National Academy of Sciences of the United States of America* 116, no. 44 (October 2019): 22212–22218; Joshua Howat Berger, "With Attention on Virus, Amazon Deforestation Surges," *Phys.Org.*, May 9, 2020.

8. Cuauhtémoc Villarreal-Treviño et al., "Larval Habitat Characterization of *Anopheles darlingi* from Its Northernmost Geographical Distribution in Chiapas, Mexico," *Malaria Journal* 14, no. 517 (December 2015); Amy Vittor et al., "Linking Deforestation to Malaria in the Amazon: Characterization of the Breeding Habitat of the Principal Malaria Vector, *Anopheles darlingi*," *American Journal of Tropical Medicine and Hygiene* 81, no. 1 (July 2009): 5–12.

9. MacDonald and Mordecai, "Amazon Deforestation Drives Malaria Transmission."

10. Oliveira-Ferreira et al., "Malaria in Brazil."

11. Others also recognize the interrelationship among ecology, human behavior, and disease. See, for example, Heather Ferguson et al., "Ecology: A Prerequisite for Malaria Elimination and Eradication," *PLoS Medicine* 7, no. 8 (August 2010); and Sebastian Funk, Marcel Salathé, and Vincent Jansen, "Modelling the Influence of Human Behavior on the Spread of Infectious Disease: A Review," *Journal of the Royal Society Interface* (May 2010): 4sif20100142.

12. Joachim Sturmberg, ed., *The Value of Systems and Complexity Sciences for Healthcare* (Heidelberg: Springer, 2016); Anthony Suchman, "Linearity, Complexity, and Well-Being," *Medical Encounter* 16, no. 4 (2002): 17–19.

13. Elizabeth Grosz philosophically unpacks how difference might be understood beyond the logic of imitation. Using the work of Henri Bergson and Gilles Deleuze, she proposes that difference arises out of a creative process of open temporal variation. See Grosz, *Becomings: Explorations in Time, Memory, and Futures* (Ithaca, NY: Cornell University Press, 1999).

14. World Health Organization, Global Health Observatory data, www.who.int/gho/hiv/en, accessed June 19, 2020.

15. Tuofu Zhu et al., "An African HIV-1 Sequence from 1959 and Implications for the Origin of the Epidemic," *Nature*, 391, no. 6667 (February 1998): 594–597; Michael Worobey et al., "Direct Evidence of Extensive HIV-1 in Kinshasa by 1960," *Nature* 455, no. 7213 (October 2008): 661–664; Tamara Giles-Vernick et al., "Social History, Biology, and the Emergence of HIV in Colonial Africa," *Journal of African History* 54, no. 1 (March 2013): 11–30; Nuno Faria et al., "The Early Spread and Epidemic Ignition of HIV-1 in Human Populations," *Science* 346, no. 6205 (October 2014): 56–61.

16. Paul Sharp and Beatrice Hahn, "Origins of HIV and the AIDS Pandemic," *Cold Spring Harbor Perspectives in Medicine* 1, no. 1 (2011): a006841.

17. Faria et al., "Early Spread."

18. Zhiwei Chen et al., "Human Immunodeficiency Virus Type 2 (HIV-2) Seroprevalence and Characterization of a Distinct HIV-2 Genetic Subtype from the Natural Range of Simian Immunodeficiency Virus-Infected Sooty Mangabeys," *Journal of Virology* 71, no. 5 (May 1997): 3953–3960.

19. Robin Weiss and Richard Wrangham, "From Pan to Pandemic," *Nature* 397, no. 6718 (February 1999): 385–386; Robin Weiss, "HIV and AIDS in Relation to Other Pandemics," EMBO reports 4, supplement 1 (June 2003): S10–S14. Although Weiss provides a useful overview in his study of the spread of HIV to the scale of a pandemic, the moralizing and judgmental undercurrent that runs throughout this essay is certainly problematic.

20. Rachael Dellar, Sarah Dlamini, and Quarraisha Abdool Karim, "Adolescent Girls and Young Women: Key Populations for HIV Epidemic Control," *Journal of the International AIDS Society* (February 2015): 64–70; Perry Halkitis, "Discrimination and Homophobia Fuel HIV Epidemic in Gay and Bisexual Men," *Psychology and AIDS Exchange Newsletter*, April 2012; Nora Volkow and Julio Montaner, "The Urgency of Providing Comprehensive and Integrated Treatment for Substance Abusers with HIV," *Health Affairs: Analysis and Commentary* 30, no. 8 (August 2011).

21. Paul Farmer, *AIDS and Accusation: Haiti and the Geography of Blame* (Berkeley: University of California Press, 2006), 259–260.

22. Thomas Gilbert et al., "The Emergence of HIV/AIDS in the Americas and Beyond," *Proceedings of the National Academy of Sciences of the United States of America* 47 (November 2007): 18566–18570.

23. U.S. Centers for Disease Control, "The Global HIV/AIDS Pandemic, 2006," *MMWR Weekly* 55, no. 31 (August 11, 2006): 841–844.

24. Gilbert et al., "Emergence of HIV/AIDS," 18566.

25. David Quammen, *Ebola: The Natural and Human History of a Deadly Virus* (New York: Norton, 2014), 3.

26. World Health Organization, "Zoonoses," July 29, 2020.

27. U.S. Centers for Disease Control and Prevention, "2014–2016 Ebola Outbreak in West Africa," March 8, 2019.

28. World Health Organization, "Origins of the 2014 Ebola Epidemic," in *One Year into the Ebola Epidemic: A Deadly, Tenacious and Unforgiving Virus,* January 2015.

29. Christina Faust et al., "Pathogen Spillover During Land Conversion," *Ecology Letters* 21, no. 4 (April 2018): 471–483; Borremans et al., "Cross-Species Pathogen Spillover"; Laura Bloomfield, Tyler McIntosh, and Eric Lambin, "Habitat Fragmentation, Livelihood Behaviors, and Contact Between People and Nonhuman Primates in Africa," *Landscape Ecology* 35 (March 2020): 985–1000.

30. Scripps Research Institute, "COVID-19 Coronavirus Epidemic Has a Natural Origin," *ScienceDaily*, March 17, 2020; David Hui et al., "The Continuing 2019-nCoV Epidemic Threat of Novel Coronaviruses to Global Health—The Latest 2019 Novel Coronavirus Outbreak in Wuhan, China," *International Journal of Infectious Diseases* 91 (January 2020): 264–266.

3. Migrations

1. Patrick Guerra, Robert Gegear, and Steven Reppert, "A Magnetic Compass Aids Monarch Butterfly Migration," *Nature Communications* 5, article no. 4164 (June 2014).

2. Tierra Curry and George Kimbrell, "Easter Monarch Butterfly Population Plunges by More Than Half: Population Overwintering in Mexico Falls Well Below Extinction Threshold," Center for Biological Diversity, March 13, 2020.

3. Lincoln Brower et al., "Oyamel Fir Forest Trunks Provide Thermal Advantages for Overwintering Monarch Butterflies in Mexico," *Insect Conservation and Diversity*, July 2009.

4. Mark Stevenson, "The World's Hunger for Avocados Is Having a Devastating Effect on Mexico," *Business Insider*, November 1, 2016.

5. Laurel Wamsley, "Sadness and Worry After 2 Men Connected to Butterfly Sanctuary Are Found Dead," National Public Radio, February 3, 2020.

6. Brower et al., "Oyamel Fir Forest Trunks Provide Thermal Advantages."

7. John Pleasants and Karen Oberhauser, "Milkweed Loss in Agricultural Fields Because of Herbicide Use: Effect on the Monarch Butterfly Population," *Insect Conservation and Diversity* 6 (2013): 135–144.

8. Karen Oberhauser, "Male Monarch Butterfly Spermatophore Mass and Mating Strategies," *Animal Behaviour* 36, no. 5 (September–October 1988): 1384–1388.

9. Anurag Agrawal, *Monarchs and Milkweed: A Migrating Butterfly, a Poisonous Plant, and Their Remarkable Story of Co-evolution* (Princeton, NJ: Princeton University Press, 2017).

10. Hidetoshi Inamine et al., "Linking the Continental Migratory Cycle of the Monarch Butterfly to Understand Its Population Decline," *Oikos* 125 (April 2016): 1081–1091.

11. Alphonso Alonso-Mejia et al., "Use of Lipid Reserves by Monarch Butterflies Overwintering in Mexico: Implications for Conservation," *Ecological Applications* 7, no. 3 (August 1997): 934–947.

12. Irepani Ruiz and his family are fictional characters based upon facts. For more on undocumented immigrant deaths in the custody of U.S. Immigration and Customs Enforcement, see Darius Tahir, " 'Black hole' of Medical Records Contributes to Deaths, Mistreatment at the Border," *Politico*, December 1, 2019.

13. Stephanie Schutze, *Constructing Transnational Political Spaces: The Multifaceted Political Activism of Mexican Migrants* (London: Palgrave Macmillan, 2016), 12.

14. ONU Mujeros, *Matrimonios y unionoes tempranas de niñas* (September 19, 2016), 6.

15. International remittances to Mexico were $35.7 billion in 2018. See Marie McAuliffe and Binod Khadria, eds., *World Migration Report 2020* (Geneva: International Organization for Migration, 2019), 3; and Kirk Semple, "Economic Freeze Cuts Remittances, a Lifeline for Migrants' Families," *New York Times*, April 25, 2020.

16. David Olson, "Duroville: Slum Mobile Home Park Finally Closes," *Press-Enterprise*, June 28, 2013.

17. Trish Hernandez and Susan Gabbard, *Findings from the National Agricultural Workers Survey (NAWS) 2015–2016: A Demographic and Employment Profile of United States Farmworkers*, research report no. 13, JBS International, January 2018.

18. Sara Quandt et al., "Workplace, Household, and Personal Predictors of Pesticide Exposure for Farmworkers," *Environmental Health Perspectives* 11, no. 6 (June 2006): 943–952.

19. United Nations, Department of Economic and Social Affairs, *Population Facts* no. 2019/4 (September 2019): 3.

20. Ana Gonzalez-Barrera and Jens Manuel Krogstad, "What We Know About Illegal Immigration from Mexico," Pew Research Center, June 28, 2019.

21. Dorian Hargrove, Tom Jones, and Mari Payton, "Customs and Border Protection Officers Now Protected from Disclosing Information to Public," February 6, 2020.

22. U.S. Customs and Border Protection, *Southwest Border Migration FY 19*, November 14, 2019.

23. Nicole Acevedo, "Why Are Migrant Children Dying in U.S. Custody?," *NBC News*, May 29, 2019.

24. Jens Manuel Krogstad, "Americans Broadly Support Legal Status for Immigrants Brought to the U.S. Illegally as Children," Pew Research Center, June 17, 2020.

25. United Nations, *Population Facts*; McAuliffe and Khadria, *World Migration Report 2020*, 2, 232.

26. McAuliffe and Khadria, *World Migration Report 2020*.

27. Data compiled by the United Nations in 2016 lists 21 percent of detected victims of trafficking being men, 49 percent women, 23 percent girls, and 7 percent boys. United Nations Office on Drugs and Crime, *Global Report on Trafficking in Persons 2018* (Vienna: UNODC Research, 2018), 10.

28. Human Rights Watch, "Rohingya."

29. Internal Displacement Monitoring Centre, *Global Report on Internal Displacement 2020*, April 2020.

30. United Nations High Commissioner for Refugees, "Frequently Asked Questions on Climate Change and Disaster Displacement," November 6, 2016.

31. United Nations World Food Programme, "FAO and WFP Concerned About the Impact of Drought on the Most Vulnerable in Central America," August 24, 2018.

32. Sarah Mahler and Dusan Ugrina, "Central America: Crossroads of the Americas," Migration Policy Institute, April 1, 2006.

33. National Aeronautics and Space Administration, *Global Warming from 1880 to 2019*, video.

34. I-Ching Chen et al., "Rapid Range Shifts of Species Associated with High Levels of Climate Warming," *Science* 333, no. 6045 (August 2011): 1024–1026.

35. World Wildlife Fund, *Monarch Butterfly* (Washington, DC: WWF, 2015).

36. David Herring, "Climate Change: Global Temperature Projections," National Oceanic and Atmospheric Administration, March 6, 2012.

37. Gretta Pecl et al., "Biodiversity Redistribution Under Climate Change: Impacts on Ecosystems and Human Well-Being," *Science* 355, no. 6332 (March 31, 2017): 2.

38. Polar and brown bear species diverged around 40,000 years ago, with polar bear genetic lineage experiencing stronger selection than that of the brown bear. See Shiping Liu et al., "Population Genomics Reveal Recent Speciation and Rapid Evolutionary Adaptation in Polar Bears," *Cell* 157, no. 4 (May 2014): 785–794; and Jodie Pongracz et al., "Recent Hybridization Between a Polar Bear and Grizzly Bears in the Canadian Arctic," *Arctic* 70, no. 2 (2017): 151–160.

39. Clint Muhlfeld et al., "Hybridization Rapidly Reduces Fitness of a Native Trout in the Wild," *Biology Letters* 5 (February 2009): 328–331.

40. Alejandro Ordonez and John Williams, "Climatic and Biotic Velocities for Woody Taxa Distributions over the Last 16,000 Years in Eastern North America," *Ecology Letters* 16 (2013): 773–781.

41. Brian Huntley, "How Plants Respond to Climate Change: Migration Rates, Individualism, and the Consequences for Plant Communities," *Annals of Botany* 67, supplement 1: *Global Change and the Biosphere* (June 1991): 15–22.

42. J. J. Lawler et al., "Projected Climate-Driven Faunal Movement Routes," *Ecology Letters* 16 (2013): 1014–1022.

4. Air

1. Carsten Egevang et al., "Tracking of Arctic Terns *Sterna paradisaea* Reveals Longest Animal Migration," *Proceedings of the National Academy of Sciences* 107, no. 5 (February 2010): 2078–2081.

2. Carsten Egevang, *Migration and Breeding Biology of Arctic Terns in Greenland* (PhD diss., Aarhus University and University of Copenhagen, 2010).

3. Egevang et al., "Tracking of Arctic Terns."

4. Jason Paur, "Red Bull Releases Incredible POV Video of 128,000-foot Stratos Jump," *Wired*, October 15, 2013.

5. Beth Dempster, "Sympoietic and Autopoietic Systems: A New Distinction for Self-Organizing Systems," University of Waterloo, School of Planning (2000), 4.

6. Dempster, "Sympoietic and Autopoietic Systems, 1.

7. Donna Harraway, "Tentacular Thinking: Anthropocene, Capitalocene, Chthulucene," in *Staying with the Trouble: Making Kin in the Chthulucene*, ed. Donna Harraway (Durham, NC: Duke University Press, 2016), 31.

8. National Aeronautics and Space Administration, "First Pictures of Earth from 100 Miles in Space, 1947," March 6, 2009.

9. Kathleen Rogers, "Fifty Years After Earthrise: The Famous Photograph Bolstered the Environmental Movement," *USA Today*, December 24, 2018.

10. Walter Benjamin, "A Short History of Photography," *Screen* 13, no. 1 (Spring 1972): 7.

11. Michael Benson, *Otherworlds: Visions of Our Solar System* (New York: Harry N. Abrams, 2017). Benson is an artist and curator. The material featured in the book was also installed in 2016 at the National History Museum, London.

12. Benjamin, "Short History of Photography," 20.

13. David Yaden et al., "The Overview Effect: Awe and Self-transcendent Experience in Space Flight," *Psychology of Consciousness: Theory, Research, and Practice* 3, no. 1 (2016): 3–4.

14. Frank White, *The Overview Effect: Space Exploration and Human Evolution* (Boston: Houghton Mifflin, 1987).

15. Yaden et al., "Overview Effect," 3.

16. Bruno Latour, "Why Gaia Is Not a God of Totality," *Theory, Culture, and Society* 34, no. 2–3 (2017): 63.

17. Henri Bergson, *Matter and Memory*, trans. N. M. Paul and W. S. Palmer (New York: Zone Books, 1990).

18. Latour, "Why Gaia Is Not a God of Totality," 62.

19. Jon Berntsen et al., *Review of Carbon Markets in 2019* (Oslo: Refinitiv, January 22, 2020); World Bank Group, *State and Trends of Carbon Pricing 2019* (Washington, DC: World Bank, Navigant, and International Carbon Action Partnership, 2019); E. Mazareanu, "Market Size of the Global

Airline Industry 2018–2021," Statista, August 18, 2021; Jon Gold, "Verizon and AT&T Billions Lead the Spending for 5G Licenses," *Networkworld*, March 13, 2020.

20. Lauri Myllyvirta, *Quantifying the Economic Costs of Air Pollution from Fossil Fuels*, Center for Research on Energy and Clean Air (February 2020), 2.

21. Congressional Research Service, *Clean Air Act: A Summary of the Act and Its Major Requirements*, RL30853 (February 25, 2020); P. St.-Laurent et al., "Impacts of Atmospheric Nitrogen Deposition on Surface Waters of the Western North Atlantic Mitigated by Multiple Feedback," *JGR Oceans* 122, no. 11 (November 2017): 8406–8426; Laurens Ganzeveld and Jos Lelieved, "Impact of Amazonian Deforestation on Atmospheric Chemistry," *Geophysical Research Letters* 31, L06105 (March 2004): 1–5; Union of Concerned Scientists, "Who's Fighting the Clean Power Plan and EPA Action on Climate Change?," April 13, 2016.

22. Anjum Hajat, Charlene Hsia, and Marie O'Neill, "Socioeconomic Disparities and Air Pollution Exposure: A Global Review," *Current Environmental Health Reports* 2 (September 2015): 440–450; LeAlan M. Jones and Lloyd Newman, *Our America: Life and Death on the South Side of Chicago* (New York: Washington Square Press, 1998); Ta-Nehisi Coates, *Between the World and Me* (New York: Random House, 2015).

23. U.S. Department of Justice, Civil Rights Division, and U.S. Attorney's Office, Northern District, *Investigation of the Chicago Police Department*, January 13, 2017; Campaign Zero (2020), "About the Data," *Mapping Police Violence*, accessed June 6, 2020.

5. Ocean

1. Gillian Mapstone, "Global Diversity and Review of Siphonophorae (Cnidaria: Hydrozoa)," *PLOS ONE* 10, no. 2 (February 2014).

2. Peter Fenner and Ian Carney, "The Irukandji Syndrome: A Devastating Syndrome Caused by a North Australian Jellyfish," *Australian Family Physician* 23, no. 11 (November 1999): 1131–1137.

3. Jonathan Lunine, *Earth: Evolution of a Habitable World*, 2nd ed. (Cambridge: Cambridge University Press, 2013); Lunine, "Physical Conditions on the Early Earth," *Philosophical Transactions of the Royal Society B: Biological Sciences* 361 (September 2006): 1721–1723.

4. Stratospheric Observatory for Infrared Astronomy (SOFIA) studies of the hyperactive 46P/Wirtanen comet show that hyperactive comets

discharge more water than regular comets as they near the sun. Given that 46P/Wirtanen has isotopic ratios similar to earth's, these findings suggest that hyperactive comets may be the source of earth's water. See Dariusz Lis et al., "Terrestrial Deuterium-to-Hydrogen Ratio in Water in Hyperactive Comets," *Astronomy Astrophysics* 625, no. L5 (May 2019): 1–8.

5. Knowing the isotope ratio between hydrogen and deuterium, Adam Sarafian and his team used this information to compare the ancient meteorite isotopic ratio with another, younger meteorite, the asteroid 4-Vesna. The asteroid formed around the same time as the earth and shares the same isotope distribution. Sarafian's findings show that 4-Vesna shares a similar hydrogen isotopic makeup to that of the ancient meteorite, making it highly likely that both the earth and 4-Vesna received their water from the same ancient source. Adam Sarafian et al., "Early Accretion of Water in the Inner Solar System from a Carbonaceous Chondrite-like Source," *Science* 346, no. 6209 (October 2014): 623–626.

6. If the ocean covers 70 percent of the earth and the earth's surface area is estimated to be 197 million square miles, this would make the ocean surface area approximately 140 million square miles.

7. Terence Hughes, J. Kerry, and T. Simpson, "Large-Scale Bleaching of Corals on the Great Barrier Reef," *Ecology* 99, no. 2 (November 2017): 501.

8. John O'Mahony et al. *At What Price? The Economic, Social and Icon Value of the Great Barrier Reef* (Brisbane: Deloitte Access Economics), 3.

9. James Lovelock, *Gaia: A New Look at Life on Earth*, 3rd rev. ed. (Oxford: Oxford University Press, 2000), 87.

10. The Gimuy Yindinji story of the reef's formation has been passed down over thousands of years, from one generation to the next, through song, dance, and ritual. Sharing any creation stories from the Dreamtime requires permission from Aboriginal elders. Out of respect for Aboriginal and Torres Strait Islander culture, I have not included the reef creation story.

11. Jeremy Beckett, *Torres Strait Islanders: Custom and Colonialism* (Cambridge: Cambridge University Press, 1987).

12. Bronwyn Fredericks, " 'We Don't Leave Our Identities at the City Limits': Aboriginal and Torres Strait Islander People Living in Urban Localities," *Australian Aboriginal Studies* 2013, no. 1 (Spring 2013): 4–16; Jennifer Sabbioni, Kay Schaffer, and Sidonie Smith, eds., *Indigenous Australian Voices: A Reader* (New Brunswick, NJ: Rutgers University Press, 1998).

13. Michael Liddle and Alice Kay, "Resistance, Survival, and Recovery of Trampled Corals on the Great Barrier Reef," *Biological Conservation* 42, no. 1 (1987): 1–18.

14. Timothy Gordon, et al., "Acoustic Enrichment Can Enhance Fish Community Development on Degraded Coral Reef Habitat," *Nature Communications* 10, no. 5414 (November 2019).

15. Jacqueline Webb, Richard Fay, and Arthur Popper, eds., *Fish Bioacoustics* (New York: Springer, 2008).

16. Marian Hu et al., "Acoustically Evoked Potentials in Two Cephalopods Inferred Using the Auditory Brainstem Response (ABR) Approach," *Comparative Biochemistry and Physiology, Part A* 153 (2009): 278–283.

17. Michael Qin et al., "Human Underwater and Bone Conduction Hearing in the Sonic and Ultrasonic Range," *Journal of the Acoustical Society of America* 129, no. 2485 (April 2011).

18. Whitlow Au, *The Sonar of Dolphins* (New York: Springer, 1993); Peter Tyack and Christopher Clark, "Communication and Acoustic Behavior of Dolphins and Whales," in *Hearing by Whales and Dolphins*, ed. Witlow Au and Richard Fay (New York: Springer, 2000), 156–224.

19. Roger Payne and Scott McVay, "Songs of Humpback Whales," *Science* 173, no. 3997 (September 1971): 585–597; Roger Payne, *Among Whales* (New York: Scribner, 1995); Mark McDonald, Sarah Resnick, and John Hildebrand, "Biogeographic Characterization of Blue Whale Song Worldwide: Using Song to Identify Populations," *Journal of Cetacean Research Management* 8, no. 1 (2006): 56.

20. Margaret Grebowicz, *Whale Song* (New York: Bloomsbury, 2017), 4; and McDonald, Resnick, and Hildebrand, "Biogeographic Characterization."

21. The moratorium on whaling went into effect in 1986. International Whaling Commission, "Commercial Whaling."

22. Jenny Allen et al., "Network Analysis Reveals Underlying Syntactic Features in a Vocally Learnt Mammalian Display, Humpback Whale Song," *Proceedings of the Royal Society B: Biological Sciences* 286, no. 1917 (December 2019): 20192014; Clare Owen et al., "Migratory Convergence Facilitates Cultural Transmission of Humpback Whale Song," *Royal Society Open Science* 6, no. 9 (September 2019): 190337.

23. Arthur Popper and Anthony Hawkins, eds., *The Effects of Noise on Aquatic Life* (New York: Springer, 2012); Callum Roberts, *The Ocean of Life: The Fate of Man and the Sea* (New York: Viking, 2012), 165–179.

24. Ronaldo Filadelfo et al., "Strandings: What Do the Historical Data Show?," *Aquatic Mammals* 35, no. 4 (December 2009): 435–444.

25. Jenna Jambeck et al., "Plastic Waste Inputs from Land into the Ocean," *Science* 347, no. 6223 (February 2015): 768–771.

26. Matthew Savoca et al., "Marine Plastic Debris Emits a Keystone Infochemical for Olfactory Foraging Seabirds," *Science Advances* 2, no. 11

(November 2016): e16000395; Natasha Daly, "Why Do Ocean Animals Eat Plastic?," *National Geographic*, December 5, 2019.

27. Peter Davidson and Rebecca Ash, "Plastic Ingestion by Mesopelagic Fishes in the North Pacific Subtropical Gyre," *Marine Ecology Progress Series* 432 (June 2013): 173–180.

28. National Oceanic and Atmospheric Administration, National Ocean Service, "How Deep Is the Ocean?"

29. Jim Clash, "Businessman Victor Vescovo Sets New World Depth Record for Mariana Trench Dive," *Forbes*, May 14, 2019; Amy Gunia, "An Explorer Just Made the Deepest Ever Manned Sea Dive—and He Found a Plastic Bag," *Time*, May 13, 2019.

30. William McDonough and Michael Braungart, *Cradle to Cradle: Remaking the Way We Make Things* (New York: Northpoint Press, 2002), 27.

31. Technological advances may enable commercial fishing fleets to increase their catch, but bottom trawling decimates ocean habitats, creating dead zones emptied of marine life. See Food and Agriculture Organization of the United Nations, *The State of World Fisheries and Aquaculture: Meeting the Sustainable Development Goals* (Rome: FAO, 2018), 4; and Madeleine Smith et al., "Microplastics in Seafood and the Implications for Human Health," *Current Environmental Health Reports* 5 (August 2018): 375–386.

6. Ice

1. Anthony Pagano et al., "Long-Distance Swimming Polar Bears (*Ursus maritimus*) of the Southern Beaufort Sea During Years of Extensive Open Water," *Canadian Journal of Zoology* 90, no. 5 (2012): 663–676.

2. Ron Togunov, Andrew Derocher, and Nicolas Lunn, "Windscapes and Olfactory Foraging in a Carnivore," *Scientific Reports* 7 (April 2017): 46332.

3. Anthony Pagano et al., "High-Energy, High-Fat Lifestyle Challenges an Arctic Apex Predator, the Polar Bear," *Science* 359, no. 6375 (February 2018): 568–572.

4. Andrew von Duyke et al., "Ringed Seal (*Pusa hispida*) Seasonal Movements, Diving, and Haul-Out Behavior in the Beaufort, Chukchi, and Bering Seas (2011–2017)," *Ecology and Evolution* 10, no. 12 (2020): 5595–5616.

5. Andrew Derocher, *Polar Bears: A Complete Guide to their Biology and Behavior* (Baltimore: Johns Hopkins University Press, 2012).

6. Polar bears have anywhere from thirty-four to forty-two teeth, including incisors, canines, premolars, and molars. Derocher, *Polar Bears*.

7. Kate Lillie et al., "Development of On-Shore Behavior Among Polar Bears (*Ursus Maritimus*) in the Southern Beaufort Sea: Inherited or Learned?," *Ecology and Evolution* 8, no. 16 (August 2018): 7791.

8. Eric Regehr, Steven Amstrup, and Ian Stirling, *Polar Bear Population Status in the Southern Beaufort Sea*, open file report 2006-1337 (US Department of the Interior and US Geological Survey, 2006), 11.

9. Elizabeth Logerwell and Kimberly Rand, *Beaufort Sea Marine Fish Monitoring 2008: Pilot Survey and Test of Hypotheses*, BOEMRE 2010-048 (Seattle, WA: Alaska Fisheries Science Center, NOAA National Marine Fisheries Service, January 2010), 5.

10. P. Lemke et al., "Observations: Changes in Snow, Ice, and Frozen Ground," in *Climate Change 2007: The Physical Science Basis*, ed. S. Solomon et al., 337–384 (Cambridge: Cambridge University Press, 2007); Johanna Laybourn-Parry, Andrew Hodson, and Martyn Tranter, *The Ecology of Snow and Ice Environments* (Oxford: Oxford University Press 2012), 1.

11. Sarah Yoder, *Assessment of the Potential Health Impacts of Climate Change in Alaska*, State of Alaska Epidemiology Bulletin, Department of Health and Social Services (January 8, 2018): vi.

12. The exact percentage of the areas of September Arctic sea ice decline from 2001 to 2013 was recorded at 24.3%, with an overall annual decline of 6%. See Walter Meier et al., "Arctic Sea Ice in Transformation: A Review of Recent Observed Changes and Impacts on Biology and Human Activity," *Review of Geophysics* 52, no. 3 (September 2014): 187.

13. On estimates that the Arctic will no longer have September sea ice by 2100, see Julien Boe, Alex Hall, and Xin Qu, "September Sea-Ice Cover in the Arctic Projected to Vanish by 2100," *Nature Geoscience* 2 (2009): 341–343. On predictions this could occur as early as 2041 to 2060, see F. Massonnet et al., "Constraining Projections of Summer Arctic Sea Ice," *Cryosphere* 6, no. 6 (November 2012): 1383–1394.

14. Claire Parkinson, "A 40-year Record Reveals Gradual Antarctic Sea Ice Increases Followed by Decreases at a Rate Exceeding the Rates Seen in the Arctic," *Proceedings of the National Academy of Sciences of the United States of America* 116, no. 29 (July 2019): 14414–14423.

15. Judah Cohen et al., "Recent Arctic Amplification and Extreme Mid-latitude Weather," *Nature Geoscience* 7, no. 9 (2014): 627; Judah Cohen, Karl Pfeiffer, and Jennifer A. Francis, "Warm Arctic Episodes Linked

with Increased Frequency of Extreme Winter Weather in the United States," *Nature Communications* 9, article number 869 (2018); Rick Thoman and John Walsh, *Alaska's Changing Environment: Documenting Alaska's Physical and Biological Changes Through Observations* (Fairbanks: International Research Center, University of Alaska, 2019), 8–9.

16. Cohen et al., "Recent Arctic Amplification"; Aiguo Dai et al., "Arctic Amplification Is Caused by Sea-Ice Loss Under Increasing CO_2," *Nature Communications* 10, article no. 121 (2019).

17. Jennifer Francis and Stephen Vavrus, "Evidence Linking Arctic Amplification to Extreme Weather in Mid-latitudes," *Geophysical Research Letters* 39, no. 6 (March 2012): L06801 1–6; and Charles Kennel and Elena Yulaeva, "Influence of Arctic Sea-Ice Variability on Pacific Trade Winds," *Proceedings of the National Academy of Sciences of the United States of America* 117, no. 6 (February 2020): 2824–2834.

18. Eric Post et al., "The Polar Regions in a 2°C Warmer World," *Science Advances* 5, no. 12 (December 2019): eeaw9883.

19. Oleg Anisimov and Frederick Nelson, "Permafrost Distribution in the Northern Hemisphere Under Scenarios of Climatic Change," *Global and Planetary Change* 14, no. 1–2 (August 1996): 59–72.

20. Methane has thirty-three times more impact on the earth's atmosphere than carbon dioxide. Drew Shindell et al., "Improved Attribution of Climate Forcing Emissions," *Science* 326, no. 5953 (October 2009): 716–718.

21. Andrew MacDougall, Christopher Avis, and Andrew Weaver, "Significant Contribution to Climate Warming from the Permafrost Carbon Feedback," *Nature Geoscience* 5, no. 10 (October 2012): 719. A petagram, also referred to as a gigaton, is equivalent to 1 billion metric tons.

22. "This feedback could result in an additional warming of 0.13–1.69°C by 2300." MacDougall, Avis, and Weaver, "Significant Contribution," 719. See also Kevin Schaefer et al., "The Impact of the Permafrost Carbon Feedback on Global Climate," *Environmental Research Letters* 9, no. 8 (August 2014): 1–9.

23. Lemke et al., "Observations," 339–340.

24. Esau Sinnok, "My World Interrupted," U.S. Department of the Interior blog, December 8, 2015.

25. Giovanni Strona and Corey J. A. Bradshaw, "Co-extinctions Annihilate Planetary Life During Extreme Environmental Change," *Scientific Reports* 8, article no. 16724 (November 13, 2018).

26. Post et al. "Polar Regions in a 2°C Warmer World."

27. Gilles Deleuze, *Difference and Repetition*, trans. Paul Patton (New York: Columbia University Press, 1994).

28. The World Meteorological Organization convened the First World Climate Conference in Geneva in February 1979. See John Zillman, "A History of Climate Activities," *World Meteorological Organization Bulletin* 58, no. 3 (July 2009). The United States ratified the 2015 Paris Climate Agreement on September 3, 2016. See United Nations Treaty Collection, "Chapter 27: Environment—7.d., Paris Agreement, Paris, 12 December 2015."

29. Robert Watson et al., *The Truth Behind the Climate Pledges* (Buenos Aires: Fundación Ecológica Universal FEU-US, December 2019), ii.

30. Adrian Parr, producer, *Thirsty and Drowning in America*, Intimate Realities of Water Project.

31. This story is a combination of several stories that different members of the community shared with me when I conducted site visits on the water challenges Native American communities face. I would like thank the residents of Shishmaref for sharing their memories, traditions, and beliefs with me.

32. Henry Huntington, Mark Nelson, and Lori Quakenbush, *Traditional Knowledge Regarding Ringed Seals, Bearded Seals, and Walrus Near Shishmaref, Alaska* (Fairbanks: Alaska Department of Fish and Game, 2016).

7. Animalia

1. One of the most influential texts extending the theory of narcissism beyond that of individual pathology and into the realm of the social is Christopher Lasch, *The Culture of Narcissism: American Life in an Age of Diminishing Expectations* (New York: Norton, 1979). For research on the connection between narcissism, social media, and selfie postings, see Ryan Brown and Virgil Zeigler-Hill, "Narcissism and the Nonequivalence of Self-Esteem Measures: A Matter of Dominance?," *Journal of Research in Personality* 36, no. 6 (December 2004): 585–592; Piotr Sorokowski et al., "Selfie Posting Behaviors Are Associated with Narcissism Among Men," *Personality and Individual Differences* 85 (October 2015): 123–127; and Roberta Biolcati, Stefano Passini, and Jens F. Binder, "Narcissism and Self-Esteem: Different Motivations for Selfie Posting Behaviors," *Cogent Psychology* 5, no. 1 (February 2018).

2. Craig Bohren and Joseph Sardie, "Utilization of Solar Radiation by Polar Animals: An Optical Model for Pelts; an Alternative Explanation," *Applied Optics* 20, no. 11 (1981): 1894–1896.

3. China Cetacean Alliance, "2018 China Cetacean Alliance Investigation into Guangzhou Grandview Aquarium, China," July 17, 2018.

4. Putting aside scientific differences about what constitutes a species, analysis of microbial and macrobial data indicates that there are nearly 1 trillion species on earth. See Kenneth Locey and Jay Lennon, "Scaling Laws Predict Global Microbial Diversity," *Proceedings of the National Academy of Sciences of the United States of America* 113, no. 21 (2016): 5970–5975.

5. Didi Kirsten Tatlow, "The 'Saddest' Polar Bear Lives in a Mall in China," *New York Times*, October 25, 2016.

6. Glenn Albrecht et al., "Solastalgia: The Distress Caused by Environmental Change," *Australasian Psychiatry* 15 (2007): S95–S98. See also Aldo Leopold, *A Sand County Almanac* (New York: Oxford University Press, 1949); Gregory Bateson, *Steps to an Ecology of Mind: Collected Essays in Anthropology, Psychiatry, Evolution, and Epistemology* (London: Paladin, 1972; Rachel Carson, *Silent Spring* (Harmondsworth, UK: Penguin, 1962); and Phyllis Windle, "The Ecology of Grief," *Bioscience* 42, no. 5 (1992): 363–366.

7. Albrecht et al., "Solastalgia," S95.

8. Svetlana Boym, *The Future of Nostalgia* (New York: Basic Books, 2001), xviii.

9. Boym, *Future of Nostalgia*, 23–30.

10. Glenn Albrecht, "Negating Solastalgia: An Emotion Revolution from the Anthropocene to the Symbiocene," *American Imago* 77, no. 1 (Spring 2020): 11–13.

11. It is important to note that environmental value for Indigenous groups also extends far beyond the neoliberal market confines of an ecosystem service. See Marcia Langton, "Burning Questions: Emerging Environmental Issues for Indigenous Peoples in Northern Australia," Center for Indigenous Natural and Cultural Resource Management, Northern Territory University, 1998; Langton, "Anthropology, Politics, and the Changing World of Aboriginal Australians," *Anthropological Forum* 21, no. 1 (2011): 1–22; Siegfried Wiessner, "The Cultural Rights of Indigenous Peoples: Achievements and Continuing Challenges," *European Journal of International Law* 22, no. 1 (February 2011): 121–140; Marc Fonda, ed., "Traditional Knowledge, Spirituality, and Lands," special issue, *International Indigenous Policy Journal* 2, no. 4 (2011); and James Phillips, "The Rights of Indigenous Peoples Under International Law," *Global Bioethics* 26 (May 2015): 120–127.

12. See Robert Brightman, *Grateful Prey: Rock Cree Human–Animal Relationships* (Oakland: University of California Press, 1993); and John

Grimm, ed., *Indigenous Tradition and Ecology* (Cambridge, MA: Harvard Center for the Study of World Religions, 2001).

13. Deborah Rose, Diana James, and Christine Watson, *Indigenous Kinship with the Natural World in New South Wales* (Huntsville: NSW National Parks and Wildlife Service, 2003).

14. Responding to the synthetic role habit plays in David Hume's view of the subject, Gilles Deleuze speaks of the "dynamic unity of habit and tendency, this synthesis of a past and a present which constitutes the future, and the synthetic identity of a past experience and of an adaption to the present." Like Hume, Deleuze maintains that it is not memory that synthesizes time; rather, memory reproduces "different structures of the given." Instead, he points to habit as that "which presents itself as a synthesis," for it "belongs to the subject." Deleuze, *Empiricism and Subjectivity: An Essay on Hume's Theory of Human Nature*, trans. Constantin Boundas (New York: Columbia University Press, 1991), 94.

15. Mark Blumberg, *Basic Instinct: The Genesis of Behavior* (New York: Thunder's Mouth Press, 2006), 83.

16. Among the many meanings of *instinct*, Patrick Bateson lists "innate, not learned, unchanged once developed, shared by all members of the species, controlled by a distinct neural module, genetically determined, and adapted during evolution." Blumberg, *Basic Instinct*, 147.

17. The ontology of difference that Deleuze outlines recognizes these two functions of repetition. One is formation of a habit through repetition of the same. The other invokes a force of differentiation, whereby difference arises through the process of repetition. See Deleuze, *Difference and Repetition*, trans. Paul Patton (New York: Columbia University Press, 1994).

18. Jack Hailman, "How an Instinct Is Learned," *Scientific American* 221, no. 6 (1969): 98–106.

19. Blumberg, *Basic Instinct*, 205.

20. Gilles Deleuze and Felix Guattari, *Anti-Oedipus: Introduction to Capitalism and Schizophrenia*, trans. Robert Hurley, Mark Seem, and Helen R. Lane (Minneapolis: University of Minnesota Press, 1983), 4.

21. Blumberg, *Basic Instinct*, 148.

22. Rachel Becker, "4 Ways Polar Bears Are Dealing with Climate Change," *National Geographic*, September 4, 2015.

23. Andrew Derocher, Nicholas Lunn, and Ian Stirling, "Polar Bears in a Warming Climate," *Integrative and Comparative Biology* 44 (2004): 163.

24. A concrete example of the inhumane weight humanity bears comes in the form of ecological grief. A growing number of climate scientists

report depression and anxiety as they witness the devastating loss of species and the damage climate change is inflicting. See Gaia Vince, "How Scientists Are Coping with 'Ecological Grief,'" *Guardian*, January 12, 2020; and David Corn, "The End of the World as They Know It," *Mother Jones*, July 8, 2019.

25. Sanja Kapidzic, "Narcissism as a Predictor of Motivations Behind Facebook Profile Picture Selection," *Cyberpsychology, Behavior, and Social Networking* 16, no. 1 (December 2012): 14–19.

26. Martin Heidegger, "The Age of the World Picture," in *The Question Concerning Technology and Other Essays*, trans. William Lovitt (New York: Harper and Row, 1977), 127–128.

27. Ian Buchanan, "At the Mall with Fish," *Australian Humanities Review*, no. 67 (November 2020): 1–16.

28. Jacques Derrida, *The Animal That Therefore I Am*, trans. David Wills (New York: Fordham University Press, 2008), 10, 25.

29. Derrida, *Animal That Therefore I Am*, 26.

30. See Alexander Plavevski, *"World's Saddest Polar Bear" at a Mall in Guangzhou, Guangdong Province, China*, Shutterstock, July 21, 2016; John Molloy, "World's Saddest Polar Bear Kept in Shopping Center Finally Sees Sunlight," *Telegraph*, November 14, 2016; and Mark Molloy, "'World's Saddest Polar Bear' Kept in Shopping Centre Finally Sees Some Sunlight," *Telegraph*, November 14, 2016.

31. Derrida, *Animal That Therefore I Am*, 16.

32. Derrida, *Animal That Therefore I Am*, 4, 21, 69.

33 Jacques Derrida, "The Animal That Therefore I Am (More to Follow)," trans. David Wills, *Critical Inquiry* 28, no. 2 (Winter 2002): 382.

34. Kay Prüfer et al., "The Bonobo Genome Compared with the Chimpanzee and Human Genomes," *Nature* 486 (June 13, 2012): 527–531.

35. Derrida also references animal experimentation, factory farming, cloning, and artificial insemination. See Derrida, *Animal That Therefore I Am*, 13, 25.

8. Eco-ontology

1. Elizabeth Kolbert, *The Sixth Extinction: An Unnatural History* (London: Bloomsbury, 2014), 268.

2. Connor Nolan et al., "Past and Future Global Transformation of Terrestrial Ecosystems Under Climate Change," *Science* 361, no. 6405 (August 2018): 920–923, at 920.

3. S. Díaz et al., eds., *The Global Assessment Report on Biodiversity and Eco-system Services: Summary for Policymakers* (Bonn: Intergovernmental Science-Policy Platform on Biodiversity and Ecosystem Services, 2019), 11, 28.

4. Naomi Klein, *This Changes Everything: Capitalism vs. The Climate* (New York: Simon and Schuster, 2014); John Bellamy Foster, Brett Clark, and Richard York, *The Ecological Rift: Capitalism's War on the Earth* (New York: Monthly Review Press, 2010); John Bellamy Foster and Brett Clark, *The Robbery of Nature: Capitalism and the Ecological Rift* (New York: Monthly Review Press, 2020); George Monbiot, *How Did We Get Into This Mess? Politics, Equality, Nature* (London: Verso, 2016); Monbiot, *Out of the Wreckage: A New Politics for an Age of Crisis* (London: Verso, 2017); Adrian Parr, *Hijacking Sustainability* (Cambridge, MA: MIT Press, 2009); Parr, *The Wrath of Capital: Neoliberalism and Climate Change Politics* (New York: Columbia University Press, 2013); Parr, *Birth of a New Earth: The Radical Politics of Environmentalism* (New York: Columbia University Press, 2017).

5. Bruno Latour, "What Protective Measures Can You Think of So We Don't Go Back to the Pre-crisis Production Model?," trans. Stephen Muecke. Originally published March 29, 2020.

6. National Aeronautics and Space Administration/Goddard Space Flight Center, "Environmental Impacts of the COVID-19 Pandemic, as Observed from Space," *ScienceDaily*, December 8, 2020.

7. Latour, "What Protective Measures."

8. Adrian Parr, "Green Scare," *Philosophy Today* 59, no. 4 (Fall 2015): 671–683.

9. James Lovelock, *The Revenge of Gaia: Earth's Climate Crisis and the Fate of Humanity* (New York: Basic Books, 2007), 141.

10. Polly Higgins, *Eradicating Ecocide*, 2nd ed. (London: Shepheard-Walwyn, 2015), 57, 63. Emphasis in original.

11. Judith Butler, *The Force of Nonviolence: An Ethico Political Bind* (London: Verso, 2020).

12. Brad Evans and Julian Reid, *Resilient Life: The Art of Living Dangerously* (London: Polity, 2014); Brad Evans and Henry Giroux, *Disposable Futures: The Seduction of Violence in the Age of Spectacle* (San Francisco: City Lights, 2015); Brad Evans and Natasha Lennard, *Violence: Humans in Dark Times* (San Francisco: City Lights, 2018).

13. Henry Giroux, *The Violence of Organized Forgetting: Thinking Beyond America's Disimagination Machine* (San Francisco: City Lights, 2014); and Giroux, "Pedagogy Against the Dead Zones of the Imagination,"

Transformations: The Journal of Inclusive Scholarship and Pedagogy 26, no. 1 (2016): 26–30.

14. Santiago Zabala, *Being at Large: Freedom in the Age of Alternative Facts* (New York: Columbia University Press, 2020).

15. Shannon Biggs, "When Rivers Hold Legal Rights: New Zealand and India Recognize Personhood for Ecosystems," *Earth Island Journal*, April 17, 2017.

16. United Nations, Department of Public Information, "Press Conference by Bolivia on New Constitution," News and Media Division, New York, January 27, 2009.

17. Parr, *Birth of a New Earth*.

18. Rosi Braidotti, *Metamorphoses: Towards a Materialist Theory of Becoming* (Cambridge: Polity, 2002); Braidotti, *The Posthuman* (Cambridge: Polity, 2013).

19. Braidotti, *Posthuman*; Butler, *Force of Nonviolence*; Bruno Latour, *Facing Gaia: Eight Lectures on the New Climatic Regime*, trans. Catherine Porter (Cambridge: Polity, 2017); Parr, *Birth of a New Earth*.

Bibliography

Acevedo, Nicole. "Why Are Migrant Children Dying in U.S. Custody?" *NBC News*, May 29, 2019. https://www.nbcnews.com/news/latino/why-are -migrant-children-dying-u-s-custody-n1010316.

Agrawal, Anurag. *Monarchs and Milkweed: A Migrating Butterfly, a Poisonous Plant, and Their Remarkable Story of Co-evolution.* Princeton, NJ: Princeton University Press, 2017.

Albrecht, Glenn. "Negating Solastalgia: An Emotion Revolution from the Anthropocene to the Symbiocene." *American Imago* 77, no. 1 (Spring 2020): 9–30.

Albrecht, Glenn, Gina-Maree Sartore, Linda Connor, Nick Higginbotham, Sonia Freeman, Brian Kelly, Helen Stain, Anne Tonna, and Georgia Pollard. "Solastalgia: The Distress Caused by Environmental Change." *Australasian Psychiatry* 15 (2007): S95–S98.

Allen, Jenny, Ellen Garland, Rebecca Dunlop, and Michael Noad. "Network Analysis Reveals Underlying Syntactic Features in a Vocally Learnt Mammalian Display, Humpback Whale Song." *Proceedings of the Royal Society B: Biological Sciences* 286, no. 1917 (December 2019): 20192014.

Alonso-Mejia, Alphonso, Eduardo Rendon-Salinas, Eneida Montesinos-Patino, and Lincoln Brower. "Use of Lipid Reserves by Monarch Butterflies Overwintering in Mexico: Implications for Conservation." *Ecological Applications* 7, no. 3 (August 1997): 934–947.

Amazon Watch. "Another Amazonian Indigenous Leader Is Murdered in Brazil." Press release, March 31, 2020. https://amazonwatch.org/news/2020 /0331-another-amazonian-indigenous-leader-is-murdered-in-brazil.

Anisimov, Oleg, and Frederick Nelson. "Permafrost Distribution in the Northern Hemisphere Under Scenarios of Climatic Change." *Global and Planetary Change* 14, no. 1–2 (August 1996): 59–72.

Appalachian Regional Commission. "ARC Announces $3.3 Million to Continue Economic Growth in Region's Coal-Impacted Communities." February 12, 2020. https://www.arc.gov/news/article.asp?ARTICLE_ID=690.

Au, Whitlow. *The Sonar of Dolphins*. New York: Springer, 1993.

Barad, Karen. *Meeting the Universe Halfway: Quantum Physics and the Entanglement of Matter and Meaning*. Durham, NC: Duke University Press, 2007.

Barkley, Anne, Joseph M. Prospero, Natalie Mahowald, Douglas S. Hamilton, Kimberly J. Popendorf, Amanda M. Oehlert, et al. "African Biomass Burning Is a Substantial Source of Phosphorus Deposition to the Amazon, Tropical Atlantic Ocean, and Southern Ocean." *Proceedings of the National Academy of Sciences* 116, no. 33 (August 2019): 16216–16221.

Bateson, Gregory. *Steps to an Ecology of Mind: Collected Essays in Anthropology, Psychiatry, Evolution, and Epistemology*. London: Paladin, 1972.

Becker, Rachel. "4 Ways Polar Bears Are Dealing with Climate Change." *National Geographic*, September 4, 2015. https://www.nationalgeographic.com/news/2015/09/150904-polar-bears-dolphins-seals-climate-change.

Beckett, Jeremy. *Torres Strait Islanders: Custom and Colonialism*. Cambridge: Cambridge University Press, 1987.

Bellamy Foster, John, and Brett Clark. *The Robbery of Nature: Capitalism and the Ecological Rift*. New York: Monthly Review Press, 2020.

Bellamy Foster, John, Brett Clark, and Richard York. *The Ecological Rift: Capitalism's War on the Earth*. New York: Monthly Review Press, 2010.

Benjamin, Walter. *Charles Baudelaire*. Trans. Harry Zohn. London: Verso, 1983.

Benjamin, Walter. "A Short History of Photography." *Screen* 13, no. 1 (Spring 1972): 5–26.

Benson, Michael. *Otherworlds: Visions of Our Solar System*. New York: Harry N. Abrams, 2017.

Berger, Joshua Howat. "With Attention on Virus, Amazon Deforestation Surges." *Phys.org*, May 9, 2020. https://phys.org/news/2020-05-attention-virus-amazon-deforestation-surges.html.

Bergson, Henri. *Matter and Memory*. Trans. N. M. Paul and W. S. Palmer. New York: Zone Books, 1990.

Berntsen, Jon, Anders Nordeng, Aje Singh Rihel, Haege Fjellheim, Lisa Zelljadt, Cathy Liao, and Maria Kolos. *Review of Carbon Markets in 2019*.

Oslo: Refinitiv, January 22, 2020. https://www.refinitiv.com/content/dam
/marketing/en_us/documents/reports/global-carbon-market-emission
-trading-system-review-2019.pdf.

Biboum, Margarita Jover, Rubén García Rubio, and Carlos Ávila Calzada. "Adrian Parr, a Polyhedral Relationship with Water." *ZARCH* 15 (December 2020): 188–195.

Biggs, Shannon. "When Rivers Hold Legal Rights: New Zealand and India Recognize Personhood for Ecosystems." *Earth Island Journal*, April 17, 2017. https://www.earthisland.org/journal/index.php/articles/entry/when _rivers_hold_legal_rights.

Biolcati, Roberta, Stefano Passini, and Jens F. Binder. "Narcissism and Self-Esteem: Different Motivations for Selfie Posting Behaviors." *Cogent Psychology* 5, no. 1 (February 2018). https://www.tandfonline.com/doi/full /10.1080/23311908.2018.1437012.

Bloomfield, Laura, Tyler McIntosh, and Eric Lambin. "Habitat Fragmentation, Livelihood Behaviors, and Contact Between People and Nonhuman Primates in Africa." *Landscape Ecology* 35 (March 2020): 985–1000.

Blumberg, Mark. *Basic Instinct: The Genesis of Behavior*. New York: Thunder's Mouth Press, 2006.

Boe, Julien, Alex Hall, and Xin Qu. "September Sea-Ice Cover in the Arctic Projected to Vanish by 2100." *Nature Geoscience* 2 (2009): 341–343.

Bohren, Craig, and Joseph Sardie. "Utilization of Solar Radiation by Polar Animals: An Optical Model for Pelts; an Alternative Explanation." *Applied Optics* 20, no. 11 (1981): 1894–1896.

Borremans, Benny, Christina Faust, Kezia Manlove, Susanne Sokolow, and James Lloyd-Smith. "Cross-Species Pathogen Spillover Across Ecosystem Boundaries: Mechanisms and Theory." *Philosophical Transactions of the Royal Society London B: Biological Sciences* 374, no. 1782 (September 2019): 20180344. https://royalsocietypublishing.org/doi/full/10.1098 /rstb.2018.0344.

Boym, Svetlana. *The Future of Nostalgia*. New York: Basic Books, 2001.

Braidotti, Rosi. *Metamorphoses: Towards a Materialist Theory of Becoming*. Cambridge: Polity, 2002.

Braidotti, Rosi. *The Posthuman*. Cambridge: Polity, 2013.

Brightman, Robert. *Grateful Prey: Rock Cree Human–Animal Relationships*. Oakland: University of California Press, 1993.

Brower, Lincoln, Ernest Williams, Daniel Slayback, Linda Fink, Isabel Ramirez, Raul Zubieta, Ivan Limon Garcia, Paul Gier, Jennifer Lear, and Tonya Van Hood. "Oyamel Fir Forest Trunks Provide Thermal

Advantages for Overwintering Monarch Butterflies in Mexico." *Insect Conservation and Diversity*, July 2009. https://onlinelibrary.wiley.com /doi/10.1111/j.1752–4598.2009.00052.x.

Brown, Ryan, and Virgil Zeigler-Hill. "Narcissism and the Non-equivalence of Self-Esteem Measures: A Matter of Dominance?" *Journal of Research in Personality* 36, no. 6 (December 2004): 585–592.

Buchanan, Ian. "At the Mall with Fish." *Australian Humanities Review*, no. 67 (November 2020): 1–16. http://australianhumanitiesreview.org/2020/11 /29/at-the-mall-with-fish.

Burnham, Robyn, and Kirk Johnson. "South American Palaeobotany and the Origins of Neotropical Rainforests." *Philosophical Transactions of the Royal Society* 359, no. 1450 (October 29, 2004): 1595–1610.

Butler, Judith. *The Force of Nonviolence: An Ethico-Political Bind*. London: Verso, 2020.

Campaign Zero. "About the Data." *Mapping Police Violence*. Accessed June 6, 2020. https://mappingpoliceviolence.org/aboutthedata.

Canning, Patrick, Sarah Rehkamp, Arnold Waters, and Hamideh Etemadnia. *The Role of Fossil Fuels in the U.S. Food System and the American Diet*. United States Department of Agriculture, Economic Research Report no. 224 (January 2017). https://www.ers.usda.gov/webdocs/publications /82194/err-224.pdf.

Carlos, Bianca, Luisa Rona, George Christophides, and Jayme Souza-Neto. "A Comprehensive Analysis of Malaria Transmission in Brazil." *Pathogens and Global Health* 113, no. 1 (February 2019): 1–13.

Carson, Rachel. *Silent Spring*. Harmondsworth, UK: Penguin, 1962.

Chen, I-Ching, Jane Hill, Ralf Ohlemuller, David Roy, and Chris Thomas. "Rapid Range Shifts of Species Associated with High Levels of Climate Warming." *Science* 333, no. 6045 (August 2011): 1024–1026.

Chen, Zhiwei, Amara Luckay, Donald Sodora, Paul Telfer, Patricia Reed, Agegnehu Gettie, James Kanu, et al. "Human Immunodeficiency Virus Type 2 (HIV-2) Seroprevalence and Characterization of a Distinct HIV-2 Genetic Subtype from the Natural Range of Simian Immunodeficiency Virus-Infected Sooty Mangabeys." *Journal of Virology* 71, no. 5 (May 1997): 3953–3960.

China Cetacean Alliance. "2018 China Cetacean Alliance Investigation into Guangzhou Grandview Aquarium, China." July 17, 2018. https:// chinacetaceanalliance.org/2018/07/17/guangzhou-grandview-aquarium.

Cilluffo, Anthony, and Neil G. Ruiz. "World's Population Is Projected to Nearly Stop Growing by the End of the Century." Pew Research Center, June 17, 2019. https://www.pewresearch.org/fact-tank/2019/06

/17/worlds-population-is-projected-to-nearly-stop-growing-by-the-end
-of-the-century.

Clash, Jim. "Businessman Victor Vescovo Sets New World Depth Record for Mariana Trench Dive." *Forbes*, May 14, 2019. https://www.forbes.com /sites/jimclash/2019/05/14/businessman-victor-vescovo-sets-new -world-depth-record-for-mariana-trench-dive/#30462880dob3.

Coates, Ta-Nehisi. *Between the World and Me*. New York: Random House, 2015.

Coble, Charles, Elaine Murray, and Dole Rice. *Earth Science*. Englewood Cliffs, NJ: Prentice-Hall, 1987.

Cohen, Judah, Karl Pfeiffer, and Jennifer A. Francis. "Warm Arctic Episodes Linked with Increased Frequency of Extreme Winter Weather in the United States." *Nature Communications* 9, article no. 869 (2018). https:// www.nature.com/articles/s41467-018-02992-9.

Cohen, Judah, James Screen, Jason Furtado, Mathew Barlow, David Whittleston, Dim Coumou, Jennifer Francis, et al. "Recent Arctic Amplification and Extreme Mid-latitude Weather." *Nature Geoscience* 7, no. 9 (2014): 627–637.

Congressional Research Service. *Clean Air Act: A Summary of the Act and Its Major Requirements*. RL30853. February 25, 2020. https://fas.org/sgp/crs /misc/RL30853.pdf.

Corn, David. "The End of the World as They Know It." *Mother Jones*, July 8, 2019. https://www.motherjones.com/environment/2019/07/weight-of-the -world-climate-change-scientist-grief.

Curry, Tierra, and George Kimbrell. "Easter Monarch Butterfly Population Plunges by More Than Half: Population Overwintering in Mexico Falls Well Below Extinction Threshold." Center for Biological Diversity, March 13, 2020. https://biologicaldiversity.org/w/news/press-releases /eastern-monarch-butterfly-population-plunges-more-half-2020-03-13.

Dai, Aiguo, Dehai Luo, Mirong Song, and Jiping Liu. "Arctic Amplification Is Caused by Sea-Ice Loss Under Increasing CO_2." *Nature Communications* 10, article no. 121 (2019). https://www.nature.com/articles/s41467-018-07954-9.

Daly, Natasha. "Why Do Ocean Animals Eat Plastic?" *National Geographic*, December 5, 2019. https://www.nationalgeographic.com/animals/2019 /12/whales-eating-plastic-pollution.

Davidson, Peter, and Rebecca Ash. "Plastic Ingestion by Mesopelagic Fishes in the North Pacific Subtropical Gyre." *Marine Ecology Progress Series* 432 (June 2013): 173–180.

De Bolle, Monica. *The Amazon Is a Carbon Bomb: How Can Brazil and the World Work Together to Avoid Setting It Off?* Policy brief. Washington, DC: Peterson Institute for International Economics, November 1, 2019.

Deleuze, Gilles. *Difference and Repetition*. Trans. Paul Patton. New York: Columbia University Press, 1994.

Deleuze, Gilles. *Empiricism and Subjectivity: An Essay on Hume's Theory of Human Nature*. Trans. Constantin Boundas. New York: Columbia University Press, 1991.

Deleuze, Gilles, and Félix Guattari. *Anti-Oedipus: Introduction to Capitalism and Schizophrenia*. Trans. Robert Hurley, Mark Seem, and Helen R. Lane. Minneapolis: University of Minnesota Press, 1983.

Dellar, Rachael, Sarah Dlamini, and Quarraisha Abdool Karim. "Adolescent Girls and Young Women: Key Populations for HIV Epidemic Control." *Journal of the International AIDS Society* (February 2015): 64–70.

De Melo, Efigenia, Carlos Alberto Cid Ferreira, and Rogerio Gribel. "A New Species of *Coccoloba* P. Browne (Polygonaceae) from the Brazilian Amazon with Exceptionally Large Leaves." *Acta Amazonica* 49, no. 4 (2019): 324–329.

Dempster, Beth. "Sympoietic and Autopoietic Systems: A New Distinction for Self-Organizing Systems." University of Waterloo, School of Planning, 2000. https://pdfs.semanticscholar.org/4429/9317a20afcd33b0a11d3b2bf4fc196088d45.pdf.

Derocher, Andrew. *Polar Bears: A Complete Guide to Their Biology and Behavior*. Baltimore: Johns Hopkins University Press, 2012.

Derocher, Andrew, Nicholas Lunn, and Ian Stirling. "Polar Bears in a Warming Climate." *Integrative and Comparative Biology* 44 (2004): 163–176.

Derrida, Jacques. *The Animal That Therefore I Am*. Trans. David Wills. New York: Fordham University Press, 2008.

Derrida, Jacques. "The Animal That Therefore I Am (More to Follow)." Trans. David Wills. *Critical Inquiry* 28, no. 2 (Winter 2002): 369–418.

Díaz, S., J. Settele, E. S. Brondízio, H. T. Ngo, M. Guèze, J. Agard, A. Arneth, et al., eds. *The Global Assessment Report on Biodiversity and Ecosystem Services: Summary for Policymakers*. Bonn: Intergovernmental Science-Policy Platform on Biodiversity and Ecosystem Services, 2019. https://doi.org/10.5281/zenodo.3553579.

Egevang, Carsten. *Migration and Breeding Biology of Arctic Terns in Greenland*. PhD diss., Aarhus University and University of Copenhagen, 2010.

Egevang, Carsten, Iain Stenhouse, Richard Phillips, Aevar Petersen, James Fox, and Janet Silk. "Tracking of Arctic Terns *Sterna paradisaea* Reveals Longest Animal Migration." *Proceedings of the National Academy of Sciences* 107, no. 5 (February 2010): 2078–2081. https://www.ncbi.nlm.nih.gov/pmc/articles/PMC2836663/#r33.

Evans, Brad, and Henry Giroux. *Disposable Futures: The Seduction of Violence in the Age of Spectacle*. San Francisco: City Lights, 2015.

Evans, Brad, and Natasha Lennard. *Violence: Humans in Dark Times*. San Francisco: City Lights, 2018.

Evans, Brad, and Julian Reid. *Resilient Life: The Art of Living Dangerously*. London: Polity, 2014.

Faria, Nuno, Andrew Rambaut, Marc Suchard, Guy Baele, Trevor Bedford, Melissa Ward, Andrew Tatem, et al. "The Early Spread and Epidemic Ignition of HIV-1 in Human Populations." *Science* 346, no. 6205 (October 2014): 56–61.

Farmer, Paul. *AIDS and Accusation: Haiti and the Geography of Blame*. Berkeley: University of California Press, 2006.

Fauset, Sophie, Michelle Johnson, Manuel Gloor, Timothy R. Baker, Abel Monteagudo, M. Roel, J. W. Brienen, et al. "Hyperdominance in Amazonian Forest Carbon Recycling." *Nature Communications* 6, article no. 6857 (April 2015). https://www.nature.com/articles/ncomms7857.

Faust, Christina, Hamish McCallum, Laura Bloomfield, Nicole Gottdenker, Thomas Gillespie, Colin Tonry, Andrew Dobson, and Raina Plowright. "Pathogen Spillover During Land Conversion." *Ecology Letters* 21, no. 4 (April 2018): 471–483.

Fenner, Peter, and Ian Carney. "The Irukandji Syndrome: A Devastating Syndrome Caused by a North Australian Jellyfish." *Australian Family Physician* 23, no. 11 (November 1999): 1131–1137.

Ferguson, Heather, Anna Dornhaus, Arlyne Beeche, Christian Borgemeister, Michael Gottlieb, Mir Mulla, John Gimnig, Durland Fish, and Gerry Killeen. "Ecology: A Prerequisite for Malaria Elimination and Eradication." *PLoS Medicine* 7, no. 8 (August 3, 2010): e1000303. https://journals.plos.org/plosmedicine/article?id=10.1371/journal.pmed.1000303.

Filadelfo, Ronaldo, Jonathan Mintz, Edward Michlovich, and Angela D'Amico. "Strandings: What Do the Historical Data Show?" *Aquatic Mammals* 35, no. 4 (December 2009): 435–444.

Fonda, Marc, ed. "Traditional Knowledge, Spirituality, and Lands." Special issue. *International Indigenous Policy Journal* 2, no. 4 (2011).

Food and Agricultural Organization of the United Nations. *Global Forest Resources Assessment 2010*, FAO Forestry Paper 163 (Rome: FAO, 2010). http://www.fao.org/3/i1757e/i1757e.pdf.

Food and Agriculture Organization of the United Nations. *The State of World Fisheries and Aquaculture: Meeting the Sustainable Development Goals*. Rome: FAO, 2018. http://www.fao.org/3/i9540en/i9540en.pdf.

Francis, Jennifer, and Stephen Vavrus. "Evidence Linking Arctic Amplification to Extreme Weather in Mid-latitudes." *Geophysical Research Letters* 39, no. 6 (March 2012): L06801.

Fredericks, Bronwyn. "'We Don't Leave Our Identities at the City Limits': Aboriginal and Torres Strait Islander People Living in Urban Localities." *Australian Aboriginal Studies* 2013, no. 1 (Spring 2013): 4–16.

Funk, Sebastian, Marcel Salathé, and Vincent Jansen. "Modelling the Influence of Human Behavior on the Spread of Infectious Disease: A Review." *Journal of the Royal Society Interface* (May 2010): 4sif20100142. https://royalsocietypublishing.org/doi/10.1098/rsif.2010.0142.

Ganzeveld, Laurens, and Jos Lelieved. "Impact of Amazonian Deforestation on Atmospheric Chemistry." *Geophysical Research Letters* 31, L06105 (March 2004).

Gaubert, Benjamin, Britton Stephens, Sourish Basu, Frederic Chevallier, Feng Deng, Eric Kort, Prabir Patra, et al. "Global Atmospheric CO_2 Inverse Models Converging on Neutral Tropical Land Exchange, but Disagreeing on Fossil Fuel and Atmospheric Growth Rate." *Biogeosciences* 16 (2019): 117–134.

Gibbs, David, Nancy Harris, and Frances Seymour. "By the Numbers: The Value of Tropical Forests in the Climate Change Equation." World Resources Institute, October 4, 2018. https://www.wri.org/blog/2018/10/numbers-value-tropical-forests-climate-change-equation.

Gilbert, Thomas, Andrew Rambaut, Gabriela Wlasiuk, Thomas Spira, Arthur Pitchenik, and Michael Worobey. "The Emergence of HIV/AIDS in the Americas and Beyond." *Proceedings of the National Academy of Sciences of the United States of America* 47 (November 2007): 18566–18570.

Giles-Vernick, Tamara, Didier Gondola, Guillaume Lachenal, and William Schneider. "Social History, Biology, and the Emergence of HIV in Colonial Africa." *Journal of African History* 54, no. 1 (March 2013): 11–30.

Giroux, Henry. "Pedagogy Against the Dead Zones of the Imagination." *Transformations: The Journal of Inclusive Scholarship and Pedagogy* 26, no. 1 (2016): 26–30

Giroux, Henry. *The Violence of Organized Forgetting: Thinking Beyond America's Disimagination Machine.* San Francisco: City Lights, 2014.

Gold, Jon. "Verizon and AT&T Billions Lead the Spending for 5G Licenses." *Networkworld*, March 13, 2020. https://www.networkworld.com/article/3532437/verizon-and-atandt-billions-lead-the-spending-for-5g-licenses.html.

Gonzalez-Barrera, Ana, and Jens Manuel Krogstad. "What We Know About Illegal Immigration from Mexico." Pew Research Center, June 28, 2019. https://www.pewresearch.org/fact-tank/2019/06/28/what-we-know -about-illegal-immigration-from-mexico.

Gordon, Timothy, Andrew Radford, Isla Davidson, Kasey Barnes, Kieran McCloskey, Sophie Nedelec, Mark Meekan, Mark McCormick, and Stephen Simpson. "Acoustic Enrichment Can Enhance Fish Community Development on Degraded Coral Reef Habitat." *Nature Communications* 10, article no. 5414 (November 2019). https://www.nature.com/articles /s41467-019-13186-2.

Grebowicz, Margaret. *Whale Song.* New York: Bloomsbury, 2017.

Grimm, John, ed. *Indigenous Tradition and Ecology.* Cambridge, MA: Harvard Center for the Study of World Religions, 2001.

Grosz, Elizabeth. *Becomings: Explorations in Time, Memory, and Futures.* Ithaca, NY: Cornell University Press, 1999.

Guerra, Patrick, Robert Gegear, and Steven Reppert. "A Magnetic Compass Aids Monarch Butterfly Migration." *Nature Communications* 5, article no. 4164 (June 2014). https://doi.org/10.1038/ncomms5164.

Gunia, Amy. "An Explorer Just Made the Deepest Ever Manned Sea Dive— and He Found a Plastic Bag. *Time,* May 13, 2019. https://time.com/5588691 /victor-vescovo-plastic-oceans.

Hailman, Jack. "How an Instinct Is Learned." *Scientific American* 221, no. 6 (1969): 98–106.

Hajat, Anjum, Charlene Hsia, and Marie O'Neill. "Socioeconomic Disparities and Air Pollution Exposure: A Global Review." *Current Environmental Health Reports* 2 (September 2015): 440–450.

Halkitis, Perry. "Discrimination and Homophobia Fuel HIV Epidemic in Gay and Bisexual Men." *Psychology and AIDS Exchange Newsletter,* April 2012. American Psychological Association. https://www.apa.org /pi/aids/resources/exchange/2012/04/discrimination-homophobia.

Hargrove, Dorian, Tom Jones, and Mari Payton. "Customs and Border Protection Officers Now Protected from Disclosing Information to Public," February 6, 2020, https://www.nbclosangeles.com/news/national-inter national/customs-and-border-protection-officers-now-protected-from -disclosing-information-to-public/2304237.

Harraway, Donna, ed. *Staying with the Trouble: Making Kin in the Chthulucene.* Durham, NC: Duke University Press, 2016.

Heidegger, Martin. "The Age of the World Picture." In *The Question Concerning Technology and Other Essays,* trans. William Lovitt, 115–154. New York: Harper and Row, 1977.

Hendryx, Michael, and Melissa M. Ahern. "Mortality in Appalachian Coal Mining Regions: The Value of Statistical Life Lost." *Public Health Reports* 124, no. 4 (July–August 2009): 541–550.

Hernandez, Trish, and Susan Gabbard. *Findings from the National Agricultural Workers Survey (NAWS) 2015–2016: A Demographic and Employment Profile of United States Farmworkers.* Research report no. 13. JBS International, January 2018. http://doleta.gov/naws/research/docs/NAWS_ Research_Report_13.pdf.

Herring, David. "Climate Change: Global Temperature Projections." National Oceanic and Atmospheric Administration, March 6, 2012. https://www.climate.gov/news-features/understanding-climate/climate -change-global-temperature-projections.

Higgins, Polly. *Eradicating Ecocide.* 2nd ed. London: Shepheard-Walwyn, 2015.

Hiwat, Helene, and Gustavo Bretas. "Ecology of *Anopheles darlingi* Root with Respect to Vector Importance: A Review." *Parasites and Vectors* 4, no. 1, article no. 177 (September 2011). https://doi.org/10.1186/1756-3305-4-177.

Hu, Marian, Hong Young Yan, Wen-Sung Chung, Jen-Chieh Shiao, and Pung-Pung Hwang. "Acoustically Evoked Potentials in Two Cephalopods Inferred Using the Auditory Brainstem Response (ABR) Approach." *Comparative Biochemistry and Physiology, Part A* 153 (2009): 278–283.

Hughes, Terence, J. Kerry, and T. Simpson. "Large-Scale Bleaching of Corals on the Great Barrier Reef." *Ecology* 99, no. 2 (November 2017): 501.

Hui, David, Esam Azhar, Tariq Madani, Francine Ntoumi, Richard Kock, Osman Dar, Giuseppe Ippolito, et al. "The Continuing 2019-nCoV Epidemic Threat of Novel Coronaviruses to Global Health—The Latest 2019 Novel Coronavirus Outbreak in Wuhan, China." *International Journal of Infectious Diseases* 91 (January 2020): 264–266.

Human Rights Watch. "Rohingya." https://www.hrw.org/tag/rohingya.

Huntington, Henry, Mark Nelson, and Lori Quakenbush. *Traditional Knowledge Regarding Ringed Seals, Bearded Seals, and Walrus Near Shishmaref, Alaska.* Fairbanks: Alaska Department of Fish and Game, 2016. https:// www.adfg.alaska.gov/static/research/programs/marinemammals/pdfs /2016_traditional_knowledge_shishmaref.pdf.

Huntley, Brian. "How Plants Respond to Climate Change: Migration Rates, Individualism and the Consequences for Plant Communities." *Annals of Botany* 67, supplement 1: *Global Change and the Biosphere* (June 1991): 15–22.

Inamine, Hidetoshi, Stephen Ellner, James Springer, and Anurag Agrawal. "Linking the Continental Migratory Cycle of the Monarch Butterfly to Understand Its Population Decline." *Oikos* 125 (April 2016): 1081–1091.

Internal Displacement Monitoring Centre. *Global Report on Internal Displacement 2020*. April 2020. https://www.internal-displacement.org/global-report/grid2020.

International Whaling Commission. "Commercial Whaling." https://iwc.int/commercial.

Jambeck, Jenna, Roland Geyer, Chris Wilcox, Theodore Siegler, Miriam Perryman, Anthony Andrady, Ramani Narayan, and Kara Lavender Law. "Plastic Waste Inputs from Land into the Ocean." *Science* 347, no. 6223 (February 2015): 768–771.

Jones, LeAlan M. and Lloyd Newman. *Our America: Life and Death on the South Side of Chicago*. New York: Washington Square Press, 1998.

Kapidzic, Sanja. "Narcissism as a Predictor of Motivations Behind Facebook Profile Picture Selection." *Cyberpsychology, Behavior, and Social Networking* 16, no. 1 (December 2012): 14–19.

Kennel, Charles, and Elena Yulaeva. "Influence of Arctic Sea-Ice Variability on Pacific Trade Winds." *Proceedings of the National Academy of Sciences of the United States of America* 117, no. 6 (February 2020): 2824–2834.

Klein, Naomi. *This Changes Everything: Capitalism vs. The Climate*. New York: Simon and Schuster, 2014.

Krogstad, Jens Manuel. "Americans Broadly Support Legal Status for Immigrants Brought to the U.S. Illegally as Children." Pew Research Center, June 17, 2020. https://www.pewresearch.org/fact-tank/2020/06/17/americans-broadly-support-legal-status-for-immigrants-brought-to-the-u-s-illegally-as-children.

Krometis, Leigh-Anne, Julia Gohlke, Korine Kolivras, Emily Satterwhite, Susan West Marmagas, and Linsey Marr. "Environmental Health Disparities in the Central Appalachian Region of the United States." *Reviews on Environmental Health* 32, no. 3 (September 2017): 253–266.

Langton, Marcia. "Anthropology, Politics, and the Changing World of Aboriginal Australians." *Anthropological Forum* 21, no. 1 (2011): 1–22.

Langton, Marcia. *Burning Questions: Emerging Environmental Issues for Indigenous Peoples in Northern Australia*. Center for Indigenous Natural and Cultural Resource Management, Northern Territory University, 1998.

Lasch, Christopher. *The Culture of Narcissism: American Life in an Age of Diminishing Expectations*. New York: Norton, 1979.

Latour, Bruno. *Facing Gaia: Eight Lectures on the New Climatic Regime*. Trans. Catherine Porter. Cambridge: Polity, 2017.

Latour, Bruno. "What Protective Measures Can You Think of So We Don't Go Back to the Pre-crisis Production Model?" Trans. Stephen Muecke. http://www.bruno-latour.fr/sites/default/files/downloads/P-202-AOC

-ENGLISH_1.pdf. Originally published in French in *AOC*, March 29, 2020.

Latour, Bruno. "Why Gaia Is Not a God of Totality." *Theory, Culture, and Society* 34, no. 2–3 (2017): 61–81.

Lawler, L. L., A. S. Ruesch, J. D. Olden, and B. H. McRae. "Projected Climate-Driven Faunal Movement Routes." *Ecology Letters* 16 (2013): 1014–1022.

Laybourn-Parry, Johanna, Andrew Hodson, and Martyn Tranter. *The Ecology of Snow and Ice Environments*. Oxford: Oxford University Press, 2012.

Lemke, P., J. Ren, R. B. Alley, I. Allison, J. Carrasco, G. Flato, Y. Fujii, et al. "Observations: Changes in Snow, Ice and Frozen Ground." In *Climate Change 2007: The Physical Science Basis*, ed. S. Solomon, D. Qin, M. Manning, Z. Chen, M. Marquis, K. B. Averyt, M. Tignor, and H. L. Miller, 337–384. Contribution of Working Group I to the Fourth Assessment Report of the Intergovernmental Panel on Climate Change. Cambridge: Cambridge University Press, 2007.

Leopold, Aldo. *A Sand County Almanac*. New York: Oxford University Press, 1949.

Liddle, Michael, and Alice Kay. "Resistance, Survival and Recovery of Trampled Corals on the Great Barrier Reef." *Biological Conservation* 42, no. 1 (1987): 1–18.

Lillie, Kate, Eric Gese, Todd Atwood, and Sarah Sonsthagen. "Development of On-Shore Behavior Among Polar Bears (*Ursus maritimus*) in the Southern Beaufort Sea: Inherited or Learned?" *Ecology and Evolution* 8, no. 16 (August 2018): 7790–7799.

Lis, Dariusz, Dominique Bockelée-Morvan, Rolf Gusten, Nicolas Biver, Jurgen Stutzki, Yan Delorme, Carlos Duran, Helmut Wiesemeyer, and Yoko Okada. "Terrestrial Deuterium-to-Hydrogen Ratio in Water in Hyperactive Comets." *Astronomy Astrophysics* 625, L5 (May 2019): 1–8.

Liu, Shiping, Eline Lorenzen, Matteo Fumagalli, Bo Li, Kelley Harris, Zijun Xiong, Long Zhou, et al. "Population Genomics Reveal Recent Speciation and Rapid Evolutionary Adaptation in Polar Bears." *Cell* 157, no. 4 (May 8, 2014): 785–794.

Locey, Kenneth, and Jay Lennon. "Scaling Laws Predict Global Microbial Diversity." *Proceedings of the National Academy of Sciences of the United States of America* 113, no. 21 (2016): 5970–5975.

Logerwell, Elizabeth, and Kimberly Rand. *Beaufort Sea Marine Fish Monitoring 2008: Pilot Survey and Test of Hypotheses*. BOEMRE 2010-048. Seattle, WA: Alaska Fisheries Science Center, NOAA National Marine Fisheries

Service, January 2010. https://www.boem.gov/sites/default/files/boem -newsroom/Library/Publications/2010/2010_048.pdf.

Lovelock, James. *Gaia: A New Look at Life on Earth*. 3rd rev. ed. Oxford: Oxford University Press, 2000.

Lovelock, James. *The Revenge of Gaia: Earth's Climate Crisis and the Fate of Humanity*. New York: Basic Books, 2007.

Lunine, Jonathan. *Earth: Evolution of a Habitable World*. 2nd cd. Cambridge: Cambridge University Press, 2013.

Lunine, Jonathan. "Physical Conditions on the Early Earth." *Philosophical Transactions of the Royal Society B: Biological Sciences* 361 (September 2006): 1721–1723.

MacDonald, Andrew, and Erin Mordecai. "Amazon Deforestation Drives Malaria Transmission, and Malaria Burden Reduces Forest Clearing." *Proceedings of the National Academy of Sciences of the United States of America* 116, no. 44 (October 2019): 22212–22218.

MacDougall, Andrew, Christopher Avis, and Andrew Weaver. "Significant Contribution to Climate Warming from the Permafrost Carbon Feedback." *Nature Geoscience* 5, no. 10 (October 2012): 719–721.

Mahler, Sarah, and Dusan Ugrina. "Central America: Crossroads of the Americas." Migration Policy Institute, April 1, 2006. https://www.migration policy.org/article/central-america-crossroads-americas.

Mapstone, Gillian. "Global Diversity and Review of Siphonophorae (Cnidaria: hydrozoa)." *PLOS ONE* 10, no. 2 (February 2014). https://journals .plos.org/plosone/article?id=10.1371/journal.pone.0087737.

Massonnet, F., T. Fichefet, H. Goosse, C. M. Bitz, G. Philippon-Berthier, M. M. Holland, and P.-Y. Barriat. "Constraining Projections of Summer Arctic Sea Ice." *Cryosphere* 6, no. 6 (November 2012): 1383–1394.

Mazareanu, E. "Market Size of the Global Airline Industry 2018–2021." Statista, August 18, 2021. Accessed October 9, 2021. https://www.statista .com/statistics/1110342/market-size-airline-industry-worldwide.

McAuliffe, Marie, and Binod Khadria, eds. *World Migration Report 2020*. Geneva: International Organization for Migration, 2019. https://www .un.org/sites/un2.un.org/files/wmr_2020.pdf.

McDonald, Mark, Sarah Resnick, and John Hildebrand. "Biogeographic Characterization of Blue Whale Song Worldwide: Using Song to Identify Populations." *Journal of Cetacean Research Management* 8, no. 1 (2006): 55–65.

McDonough, William, and Michael Braungart. *Cradle to Cradle: Remaking the Way We Make Things*. New York: Northpoint Press, 2002.

McKibben, Bill. *Earth: Making a Life on a Tough New Planet.* New York: Henry Holt, 2010.

Meier, Walter, Greta Hovelsrud, Bob van Oort, Jeffrey Key, Kit Kovacs, Christine Michel, Christian Haas, et al. "Arctic Sea Ice in Transformation: A Review of Recent Observed Changes and Impacts on Biology and Human Activity." *Review of Geophysics* 52, no. 3 (September 2014): 185–217.

Molloy, John. "World's Saddest Polar Bear Kept in Shopping Center Finally Sees Sunlight." *Telegraph,* November 14, 2016. https://www.telegraph.co .uk/news/2016/11/14/worlds-saddest-polar-bear-kept-in-shopping -centre-finally-sees-s.

Monbiot, George. *How Did We Get Into This Mess? Politics, Equality, Nature.* London: Verso, 2016.

Monbiot, George. *Out of the Wreckage: A New Politics for an Age of Crisis.* London: Verso, 2017.

Muhlfeld, Clint, Steven Kalinowski, Thomas McMahon, Mark Taper, Sally Painter, Robb Leary, and Fred Allendorf. "Hybridization Rapidly Reduces Fitness of a Native Trout in the Wild." *Biology Letters* 5 (February 2009): 328–331.

Myllyvirta, Lauri. *Quantifying the Economic Costs of Air Pollution from Fossil Fuels.* Center for Research on Energy and Clean Air, February 2020. https://energyandcleanair.org/wp/wp-content/uploads/2020/02/Cost -of-fossil-fuels-briefing.pdf.

National Aeronautics and Space Administration. "First Pictures of Earth from 100 Miles in Space, 1947." March 6, 2009. https://www.nasa.gov /multimedia/imagegallery/image_feature_1298.html.

National Aeronautics and Space Administration. *Global Warming from 1880 to 2019.* Video. https://climate.nasa.gov/climate_resources/139/video-global -warming-from-1880-to-2019.

National Aeronautics and Space Administration, Goddard Institute for Space Studies. "GISS Surface Temperature Analysis." Accessed April 26, 2020. https://data.giss.nasa.gov/gistemp/graphs.

National Aeronautics and Space Administration/Goddard Space Flight Center. "Environmental Impacts of the COVID-19 Pandemic, as Observed from Space." *ScienceDaily,* December 8, 2020. https://www.sciencedaily .com/releases/2020/12/201208162957.htm.

National Oceanic and Atmospheric Administration, National Ocean Service. "How Deep Is the Ocean?" https://oceanservice.noaa.gov/facts/ocean depth.html.

Nolan, Connor, Jonathan Overpeck, Judy Allen, Patricia Anderson, Julio Betancourt, Heather Binney, Simon Brewer, et al. "Past and Future Global Transformation of Terrestrial Ecosystems Under Climate Change." *Science* 361, no. 6405 (August 2018): 920–923.

Oberhauser, Karen. "Male Monarch Butterfly Spermatophore Mass and Mating Strategies." *Animal Behaviour* 36, no. 5 (September–October 1988): 1384–1388.

Oliveira-Ferreira, Joseli, Marcus Lacerda, Patrícia Brasil, José Ladislau, Pedro Tauil, and Cláudio Tadeu Daniel-Ribeiro. "Malaria in Brazil: An Overview." *Malaria Journal* 9, no. 115 (April 30, 2010). https://www.ncbi .nlm.nih.gov/pmc/articles/PMC2891813.

Olson, David. "Duroville: Slum Mobile Home Park Finally Closes." *Press-Enterprise*, June 28, 2013. https://www.pe.com/2013/06/28/duroville-slum -mobile-home-park-finally-closes-3.

O'Mahony, John, Ric Simes, David Redhill, Kelly Heaton, Claire Atkinson, Emily Hayward, and Mai Nguen. *At What Price? The Economic, Social and Icon Value of the Great Barrier Reef.* Brisbane: Deloitte Access Economics. https://www2.deloitte.com/au/en/pages/economics/articles/great -barrier-reef.html.

ONU Mujeros. *Matrimonios y unionoes tempranas de niñas.* September 19, 2016. http://www2.unwomen.org/-/media/field%20office%20mexico/docu mentos/publicaciones/2016/matrimonio%20infantil_.pdf?.

Ordonez, Alejandro, and John Williams. "Climatic and Biotic Velocities for Woody Taxa Distributions over the Last 16,000 Year in Eastern North America." *Ecology Letters* 16 (2013): 773–781.

Owen, Clare, Luke Rendell, Rochelle Constantine, Michael Noad, Jenny Allen, Olive Andrews, Claire Garrigue, et al. "Migratory Convergence Facilitates Cultural Transmission of Humpback Whale Song." *Royal Society Open Science* 6, no. 9 (September 2019): 190337.

Pagano, Anthony, G. M. Durner, K. D. Rode, T. C. Atwood, S. N. Atkinson, E. Peacock, and D. P. Costa. "High-Energy, High-Fat Lifestyle Challenges an Arctic Apex Predator, the Polar Bear." *Science* 359, no. 6375 (February 2018): 568–572.

Pagano, Anthony, George Durner, Kristin Simac, Geoff York, and Steven Amstrup. "Long-Distance Swimming Polar Bears (*Ursus maritumus*) of the Southern Beaufort Sea During Years of Extensive Open Water." *Canadian Journal of Zoology* 90, no. 5 (2012): 663–676.

Parkinson, Claire. "A 40-year Record Reveals Gradual Antarctic Sea Ice Increases Followed by Decreases at a Rate Exceeding the Rates Seen in the Arctic." *Proceedings of the National Academy of Sciences of the United States of America* 116, no. 29 (July 2019): 14414–14423.

Parr, Adrian. *Birth of a New Earth: The Radical Politics of Environmentalism.* New York: Columbia University Press, 2017.

Parr, Adrian. "The Great Slumber . . . and Then There Were None." *Los Angeles Review of Books,* September 9, 2019. https://thephilosophicalsalon.com /the-great-slumber-and-then-there-were-none.

Parr, Adrian. "Green Scare." *Philosophy Today* 59, no. 4 (Fall 2015): 671–683.

Parr, Adrian. *Hijacking Sustainability.* Cambridge, MA: MIT Press, 2009.

Parr, Adrian, producer. *Thirsty and Drowning in America.* Intimate Realities of Water Project. https://intimaterealitiesofwater.org/#phase2.

Parr, Adrian. *The Wrath of Capital: Neoliberalism and Climate Change Politics.* New York: Columbia University Press, 2013.

Paur, Jason. "Red Bull Releases Incredible POV Video of 128,000-Foot Stratos Jump." *Wired,* October 15, 2013. https://www.wired.com/2013/10/pov -red-bull-stratos-jump.

Payne, Roger. *Among Whales.* New York: Scribner, 1995.

Payne, Roger, and Scott McVay. "Songs of Humpback Whales." *Science* 173, no. 3997 (September 1971): 585–597.

Pecl, Gretta T., Miguel B. Araújo, Johann D. Bell, Julia Blanchard, Timothy C. Bonebrake, I-Ching Chen, Timothy D. Clark, et al. "Biodiversity Redistribution Under Climate Change: Impacts on Ecosystems and Human Well-Being." *Science* 355, no. 6332 (March 31, 2017): 1–9.

Phillips, James. "The Rights of Indigenous Peoples Under International Law." *Global Bioethics* 26 (May 2015): 120–127.

Plavevski, Alexander. *"World's Saddest Polar Bear" at a Mall in Guangzhou, Guangdong Province, China.* Shutterstock, July 21, 2016. https://www.shutterstock .com/editorial/image-editorial/worlds-saddest-polar-bear-at-a-mall-in -guangzhou-guangdong-province-china-21-jul-2016-5780229n; and https:// www.shutterstock.com/editorial/image-editorial/worlds-saddest-polar-bear -at-a-mall-in-guangzhou-guangdong-province-china-21-jul-2016-5780229c.

Pleasants, John, and Karen Oberhauser. "Milkweed Loss in Agricultural Fields Because of Herbicide Use: Effect on the Monarch Butterfly Population." *Insect Conservation and Diversity* 6 (2013): 135–144.

Pongracz, Jodie, David Paetkau, Marsha Branigan, and Evan Richardson. "Recent Hybridization Between a Polar Bear and Grizzly Bears in the Canadian Arctic." *Arctic* 70, no. 2 (2017): 151–160.

Popper, Arthur, and Anthony Hawkins, eds. *The Effects of Noise on Aquatic Life.* New York: Springer, 2012.

Post, Eric, Richard Alley, Torben Christensen, Marc Macias-Fauria, Bruce Forbes, Michael Gooseff, Amy Iler, et al. "The Polar Regions in a 2°C Warmer World." *Science Advances* 5, no. 12 (December 2019): eeaw9883. https://www.ncbi.nlm.nih.gov/pmc/articles/PMC6892626.

Pringle, Heather. "In Peril." *Science* 348, no. 6239 (June 2015): 1080–1085.

Prüfer, Kay, Kasper Munch, Ines Hellmann, Keiko Akagi, Jason R. Miller, Brian Walenz, Sergey Koren, et al. "The Bonobo Genome Compared with the Chimpanzee and Human Genomes." *Nature* 486 (June 13, 2012): 527–531. https://doi.org/10.1038/nature11128.

Qin, Michael, Derek Schwaller, Matthew Babina, and Edward Cudahy. "Human Underwater and Bone Conduction Hearing in the Sonic and Ultrasonic Range." *Journal of the Acoustical Society of America* 129, no. 2485 (April 2011). https://asa.scitation.org/doi/10.1121/1.3588185.

Quammen, David. *Ebola: The Natural and Human History of a Deadly Virus.* New York: Norton, 2014.

Quandt, Sara, Maria Hernandez-Valero, Joseph Grzywacz, Joseph Hovey, Melissa Gonzales, and Thomas Arcury. "Workplace, Household, and Personal Predictors of Pesticide Exposure for Farmworkers." *Environmental Health Perspectives* 11, no. 6 (June 2006): 943–952.

Rasmussen, Carol. "NASA Finds Good News on Forests and Carbon Dioxide." National Aeronautics and Space Administration, December 29, 2014. https://www.nasa.gov/jpl/nasa-finds-good-news-on-forests-and-carbon-dioxide.

Regehr, Eric, Steven Amstrup, and Ian Stirling. *Polar Bear Population Status in the Southern Beaufort Sea.* Open file report 2006-1337. US Department of the Interior and US Geological Survey, 2006. https://pubs.usgs.gov/of/2006/1337/pdf/ofr20061337.pdf.

Roberts, Callum. *The Ocean of Life: The Fate of Man and the Sea.* New York: Viking, 2012.

Rogers, Kathleen. "Fifty Years After Earthrise: The Famous Photograph Bolstered the Environmental Movement." *USA Today*, December 24, 2018. https://www.usatoday.com/story/opinion/2018/12/24/earthrise-50th-anniversary-photograph-earth-day-climate-change-column/240119 6002.

Rose, Deborah, Diana James, and Christine Watson. *Indigenous Kinship with the Natural World in New South Wales.* Huntsville: NSW National Parks and Wildlife Service, 2003.

Sabbioni, Jennifer, Kay Schaffer, and Sidonie Smith, eds. *Indigenous Australian Voices: A Reader.* New Brunswick, NJ: Rutgers University Press, 1998.

Sarafian, Adam, Sune Nielsen, Horst Marschall, Francis McCubbin, and Brian Monteleone. "Early Accretion of Water in the Inner Solar System from a Carbonaceous Chondrite-like Source." *Science* 346, no. 6209 (October 2014): 623–626.

Savoca, Matthew, Martha Wohlfeil, Susan Ebeler, and Gabrielle Nevitt. "Marine Plastic Debris Emits a Keystone Infochemical for Olfactory Foraging Seabirds." *Science Advances* 2, no. 11 (November 2016): e16000395. https://advances.sciencemag.org/content/2/11/e1600395.

Schaefer, Kevin, Hugues Lantuit, Vladimir Romanovsky, Edward Schuur, and Ronald Witt. "The Impact of the Permafrost Carbon Feedback on Global Climate." *Environmental Research Letters* 9, no. 8 (August 2014): 1–9. https://iopscience.iop.org/article/10.1088/1748–9326/9/8/085003/pdf.

Schutze, Stephanie. *Constructing Transnational Political Spaces: The Multifaceted Political Activism of Mexican Migrants*. London: Palgrave Macmillan, 2016.

Scripps Research Institute. "COVID-19 Coronavirus Epidemic Has a Natural Origin." *ScienceDaily*, March 17, 2020. https://www.sciencedaily.com/releases/2020/03/200317175442.htm.

Scully, Stephen. *Hesiod's Theogony: From Near Eastern Creation Myths to Paradise Lost*. Oxford: Oxford University Press, 2015.

Semple, Kirk. "Economic Freeze Cuts Remittances, a Lifeline for Migrants' Families." *New York Times*, April 25, 2020. https://www.nytimes.com/2020/04/25/world/americas/virus-migrants-mexico-remittances.html.

Sharp, Paul, and Beatrice Hahn. "Origins of HIV and the AIDS Pandemic." *Cold Spring Harbor Perspectives in Medicine* 1, no. 1 (2011): a006841.

Shindell, Drew, Gregory Faluvegi, Gavin Schmidt, Nadine Unger, and Susanne Bauer. "Improved Attribution of Climate Forcing Emissions." *Science* 326, no. 5953 (October 2009): 716–718.

Sinnok, Esau. "My World Interrupted." U.S. Department of the Interior blog, December 8, 2015. https://www.doi.gov/blog/my-world-interrupted.

Smith, Madeleine, David Love, Chelsea Rochman, and Roni Neff. "Microplastics in Seafood and the Implications for Human Health." *Current Environmental Health Reports* 5 (August 2018): 375–386.

Sorokowski, Piotr, Agnieszka Sorokowska, Anna Oleszkiewicz, Tomasz Frackowiak, A. Huk, and Katarzyna Pisanski. "Selfie Posting Behaviors Are Associated with Narcissism Among Men." *Personality and Individual Differences* 85 (October 2015): 123–127.

Stevenson, Mark. "The World's Hunger for Avocados Is Having a Devastating Effect on Mexico." *Business Insider*, November 1, 2016. https://www

.businessinsider.com/ap-mexico-deforestation-for-avocados-much
-higher-than-thought-2016-10.

St.-Laurent, P., M. A. M. Friedrichs, R. G. Najjar, D. K. Martins, M. Herrmann, S.K. Miller, and J. Wilkin. "Impacts of Atmospheric Nitrogen Deposition on Surface Waters of the Western North Atlantic Mitigated by Multiple Feedback." *JGR Oceans* 122, no. 11 (November 2017): 8406–8426.

Strona, Giovanni, and Corey J. A. Bradshaw. "Co-extinctions Annihilate Planetary Life During Extreme Environmental Change." *Scientific Reports* 8, article no. 16724 (November 13, 2018). https://www.nature.com/articles/s41598-018-35068-1.

Sturmberg, Joachim, ed. *The Value of Systems and Complexity Sciences for Healthcare.* Heidelberg: Springer, 2016.

Suchman, Anthony. "Linearity, Complexity, and Well-Being." *Medical Encounter* 16, no. 4 (2002): 17–19.

Tahir, Darius. "'Black Hole' of Medical Records Contributes to Deaths, Mistreatment at the Border." *Politico*, December 1, 2019. https://www.politico.com/news/2019/12/01/medical-records-border-immigration-074507.

Tatlow, Didi Kirsten. "The 'Saddest' Polar Bear Lives in a Mall in China." *New York Times*, October 25, 2016. https://www.nytimes.com/2016/10/26/world/asia/china-polar-bear-shopping-mall.html.

Ter Steege, Hans, Nigel C. A. Pitman, Daniel Sabatier, Christopher Baraloto, Rafael P. Salomão, Juan Ernesto Guevara, Oliver L. Phillips, et al. "Hyperdominance in the Amazonian Tree Flora." *Science* 342, no. 6156 (October 2013): 1243092.

Thoman, Rick, and John Walsh. *Alaska's Changing Environment: Documenting Alaska's Physical and Biological Changes Through Observations.* Fairbanks: International Research Center, University of Alaska, 2019.

Togunov, Ron, Andrew Derocher, and Nicolas Lunn. "Windscapes and Olfactory Foraging in a Carnivore." *Scientific Reports* 7 (April 2017): 46332. https://www.nature.com/articles/srep46332.pdf.

Tyack, Peter, and Christopher Clark. "Communication and Acoustic Behavior of Dolphins and Whales." In *Hearing by Whales and Dolphins*, ed. Witlow Au and Richard Fay, 156–224. New York: Springer, 2000.

Union of Concerned Scientists. "Who's Fighting the Clean Power Plan and EPA Action on Climate Change?" April 13, 2016. https://www.ucsusa.org/resources/whos-fighting-clean-power-plan.

United Nations, Department of Economic and Social Affairs. *Population Facts* no. 2019/4 (September 2019). https://reliefweb.int/sites/reliefweb.int/files/resources/MigrationStock2019_PopFacts_2019-04.pdf.

United Nations, Department of Public Information. "Press Conference by Bolivia on New Constitution." News and Media Division, New York, January 27, 2009. https://www.un.org/press/en/2009/090127_Bolivia .doc.htm.

United Nations Environment Programme. "Evaluate Land to Halt Annual Loss of 24 Billion Tonnes of Fertile Soil, Expert Panel Says." Press release, June 17, 2016. https://www.unenvironment.org/news-and-stories/press -release/evaluate-land-halt-annual-loss-24-billion-tonnes-fertile-soil -expert.

United Nations Forum on Forests. *United Nations Strategic Plan for Forests 2030*. Briefing note. https://www.un.org/esa/forests/wp-content/uploads /2017/09/UNSPF-Briefing_Note.pdf.

United Nations High Commissioner for Refugees. "Frequently Asked Questions on Climate Change and Disaster Displacement." November 6, 2016. https://www.unhcr.org/en-us/news/latest/2016/11/581f52dc4/frequently -asked-questions-climate-change-disaster-displacement.html.

United Nations Office on Drugs and Crime. *Global Report on Trafficking in Persons 2018*. Vienna: UNODC Research, 2018.

United Nations Treaty Collection. "Chapter 27: Environment—7.d. Paris Agreement. Paris, 12 December 2015." https://treaties.un.org/Pages/View Details.aspx?src=TREATY&mtdsg_no=XXVII-7-d&chapter=27& clang=_en.

United Nations World Food Programme. "FAO and WFP Concerned About the Impact of Drought on the Most Vulnerable in Central America." August 24, 2018. https://www.wfp.org/news/fao-and-wfp-concerned -about-impact-drought-most-vulnerable-central-america.

U.S. Centers for Disease Control and Prevention. "The Global HIV/AIDS Pandemic, 2006." *MMWR Weekly* 55, no. 31 (August 11, 2006): 841–844. https://www.cdc.gov/mmwr/preview/mmwrhtml/mm5531a1.htm.

U.S. Centers for Disease Control and Prevention. "2014–2016 Ebola Outbreak in West Africa." March 8, 2019. https://www.cdc.gov/vhf/ebola /history/2014-2016-outbreak/index.html.

U.S. Centers for Disease Control and Prevention. "Malaria: Biology." July 16, 2020. www.cdc.gov/malaria/about/biology/index.html#tabs-1-5.

U.S. Customs and Border Protection. *Southwest Border Migration FY 2019*. November 14, 2019. https://www.cbp.gov/newsroom/stats/sw-border -migration/fy-2019.

U.S. Department of Justice, Civil Rights Division and United States Attorney's Office, Northern District. *Investigation of the Chicago Police Department*. January 13, 2017. https://www.justice.gov/opa/file/925846/download.

Villarreal-Treviño, Cuauhtémoc, Patricia Penilla-Navarro, M. Guadalupe Vázquez-Martínez, David Moo-Llanes, Jana Ríos-Delgado, Ildefonso Fernández-Salas, and Américo Rodríguez. "Larval Habitat Characterization of *Anopheles darlingi* from its Northernmost Geographical Distribution in Chiapas, Mexico." *Malaria Journal* 14, no. 517 (December 2015). https://doi.org/10.1186/s12936-015-1037-0.

Vince, Gaia. "How Scientists Are Coping with 'Ecological Grief.'" *Guardian*, January 12, 2020. https://www.theguardian.com/science/2020/jan/12/how-scientists-are-coping-with-environmental-grief.

Vittor, Amy, William Pan, Robert Gilman, James Tielsch, Gregory Glass, Tim Shields, Wagner Sánchez-Lozano, et al. "Linking Deforestation to Malaria in the Amazon: Characterization of the Breeding Habitat of the Principal Malaria Vector, *Anopheles darlingi*." *American Journal of Tropical Medicine and Hygiene* 81, no. 1 (July 2009): 5–12.

Volkow, Nora, and Julio Montaner. "The Urgency of Providing Comprehensive and Integrated Treatment for Substance Abusers with HIV." *Health Affairs: Analysis and Commentary* 30, no. 8 (August 2011). https://www.healthaffairs.org/doi/10.1377/hlthaff.2011.0663.

Von Duyke, Andrew, David Douglas, Jason Herreman, and Justin Crawford. "Ringed Seal (*Pusa hispida*) Seasonal Movements, Diving, and Haul-Out Behavior in the Beaufort, Chukchi, and Bering Seas (2011–2017)." *Ecology and Evolution* 10, no. 12 (June 2020): 5595–5616.

Wamsley, Laurel. "Sadness and Worry After 2 Men Connected to Butterfly Sanctuary Are Found Dead." National Public Radio, February 3, 2020. https://www.npr.org/2020/02/03/802359415/sadness-and-worry-after-2-men-connected-to-butterfly-sanctuary-are-found-dead.

Ward, Peter. *The Medea Hypothesis: Is Life on Earth Ultimately Self-Destructive?* Princeton, NJ: Princeton University Press, 2009.

Watson, Robert, James J. McCarthy, Pablo Canziani, Nebojsa Nakicenovic, and Liliana Hisas. *The Truth Behind the Climate Pledges*. Buenos Aires: Fundación Ecológica Universal FEU-US, November 2019. https://www.researchgate.net/publication/337033405_The_Truth_Behind_the_Climate_Pledges.

Watson, Traci. "The Trickster Microbes That Are Shaking Up the Tree of Life." *Nature* 569 (May 2019): 322–324.

Webb, Jacqueline, Richard Fay, and Arthur Popper, eds. *Fish Bioacoustics*. New York: Springer, 2008.

Weiss, Robin. "HIV and AIDS in Relation to Other Pandemics." EMBO reports 4, supplement 1 (June 2003): S10–S14. https://www.ncbi.nlm.nih.gov/pmc/articles/PMC1326444.

Weiss, Robin, and Richard Wrangham. "From Pan to Pandemic." *Nature* 397, no. 6718 (February 1999): 385–386.

Weiss, Madeline, Filipa Sousa, Natalia Mrnjavac, Sinjay Neukirchen, Mayo Roettger, Shijulal Nelson-Sathi, and William Martin. "The Physiology and Habitat of the Last Universal Common Ancestor." *Nature Microbiology* 1, no. 9 (July 2016): 16116.

Welch, S. G., I. A. McGregor, and K. Williams. "The Duffy Blood Group and Malaria Prevalence in Gambian West Africa." *Transactions of the Royal Society of Tropical Medicine and Hygiene* 71, no. 4 (January 1977): 295–296.

Westenberger, Scott, Colleen McClean, Rana Chattapadhyay, Neekesh Dharia, Jane Carlton, John Barnwell, William Collins, et al. "A Systems-Based Analysis of *Plasmodium vivax* Lifecycle Transcription from Human to Mosquito." *PLOS Neglected Tropical Diseases* 4, no. 4 (April 2010). https://www.ncbi.nlm.nih.gov/pmc/articles/PMC2850316.

White, Frank. *The Overview Effect: Space Exploration and Human Evolution.* Boston: Houghton Mifflin, 1987.

Wiessner, Siegfried. "The Cultural Rights of Indigenous Peoples: Achievements and Continuing Challenges." *European Journal of International Law* 22, no. 1 (February 2011): 121–140.

Wilson, Edward O. *The Future of Life.* New York: Knopf, 2002.

Windle, Phyllis. "The Ecology of Grief." *Bioscience* 42, no. 5 (1992): 363–366.

World Bank Group. *State and Trends of Carbon Pricing 2019.* Washington, DC: World Bank, Navigant, and International Carbon Action Partnership, 2019. http://documents.worldbank.org/curated/en/191801559846379845/pdf/State-and-Trends-of-Carbon-Pricing-2019.pdf.

World Health Organization. "Origins of the 2014 Ebola Epidemic." In *One Year into the Ebola Epidemic: A Deadly, Tenacious and Unforgiving Virus.* January 2015. https://www.who.int/news-room/spotlight/one-year-into-the-ebola-epidemic/origins-of-the-2014-ebola-epidemic.

World Health Organization. "Zoonoses," July 29, 2020, https://www.who.int/topics/zoonoses/en.

World Wildlife Fund. *Monarch Butterfly.* WWF Wildlife and Climate Change Series. Washington, DC: WWF, 2015. https://c402277.ssl.cf1.rackcdn.com/publications/845/files/original/Monarch_butterfly_-_WWF_wildlife_and_climate_change_series.pdf.

World Wildlife Fund. "Inside the Amazon." https://wwf.panda.org/knowledge_hub/where_we_work/amazon/about_the_amazon.

World Wildlife Fund. "Species Directory." https://www.worldwildlife.org/species/directory.

Worobey, Michael, Marlea Gemmel, Dirk Teuwen, Tamara Haselkom, Kevin Kunstman, Michael Bunce, Jean-Jacques Muyembe, et al. "Direct Evidence of Extensive HIV-1 in Kinshasa by 1960." *Nature* 455, no. 7213 (October 2008): 661–664.

Yaden, David, Jonathan Iwry, Johannes Eichstaedt, George Vaillant, Kelley Slack, Yukun Zhao, and Andrew Newberg. "The Overview Effect: Awe and Self-transcendent Experience in Space Flight." *Psychology of Consciousness: Theory, Research, and Practice* 3, no. 1 (2016): 1–11.

Yoder, Sarah. *Assessment of the Potential Health Impacts of Climate Change in Alaska.* State of Alaska Epidemiology Bulletin, Department of Health and Social Services, January 8, 2018. https://www.commerce.alaska.gov/web /Portals/4/pub/Potential_Health_Impacts_ClimateChange1.2018.pdf.

Zabala, Santiago. *Being at Large: Freedom in the Age of Alternative Facts.* New York: Columbia University Press, 2020.

Zhu, Tuofu, Bette Korber, Andre Nahmias, Edward Hooper, Paul Sharp, and David Ho. "An African HIV-1 Sequence from 1959 and Implications for the Origin of the Epidemic." *Nature* 391, no. 6667 (February 1998): 594–597.

Zillman, John. "A History of Climate Activities." *World Meteorological Organization Bulletin* 58, no. 3 (July 2009). https://public.wmo.int/en/bulletin /history-climate-activities.

Captions

1. Land

(page 9)   Jim Bahn, "Inside of Sequoia Tree." Openverse. Licensed under CC BY 2.0.

(page 10)   Tim Green aka atoach, "Tree Stump." Openverse. Licensed under CC BY 2.0.

2. Parasite

(page 27)   NIAID, "*Anopheles stephensi* Mosquito Larvae." Openverse. Marked with a CC BY 2.0 license.

(page 28)   DFAT photo library, "HIV in Indonesia." Openverse. Licensed under CC BY 2.0.

3. Migrations

(page 45)   Peter Haden, "Central American Migrants Find Quarter in Southern Mexico." Openverse. Licensed under CC BY 2.0.

(page 46)   OakleyOriginals, "Monarch Adornment." Openverse. Licensed under CC BY 2.0.

4. Air

(page 65)   Benoit Duchatelet, "Felix Baumgartner sous voile." Openverse. Licensed under CC BY 2.0.

(page 66)   NASA Goddard Photo and Video, "Cloud Streets in Davis Strait." Openverse. Licensed under CC BY 2.0.

(page 67)   Wildlife Boy1, "Artic Tern." Openverse. Licensed under CC BY 2.0.

5. Ocean

(page 85)   ericdalecreative, "Plastic bursts from an albatross carcass as it decomposes. This particular bird had 558 pieces of plastic in its stomach when it died, which was likely the cause." Openverse. Marked with CC PDM 1.0.

(page 86)   USFWS Headquarters, "Albatross at Midway Atoll Refuge." Openverse. Licensed under CC BY 2.0.

(page 87)   Hamed Saber, "Sunset Wave or دلشوره" Openverse. Licensed under CC BY 2.0.

(page 88)   James St. John, "*Diploria strigosa* fossil symmetrical brain coral (Cockburn Town Member, Grotto Beach Formation, Upper Pleistocene, 114–127 ka; Cockburn Town Fossil Reef, San Salvador Island, Bahamas) 3." Openverse. Licensed under CC BY 2.0.

(page 89)   minicooper93402, "Blue Whale (*Balaenoptera musculus*)—so dark—i wasn't going to post, but i was so happy to see a blue!" Openverse. Licensed under CC BY 2.0.

6. Ice

(page 107)   feverblue, "Polar Bears." Openverse. Licensed under CC BY-SA 2.0.

(page 108)   D-Stanley, "Southern Ocean Iceberg." Openverse. Licensed under CC BY 2.0.

7. Animalia

(page 125)   JordanAnthony, "Polar Bear." Openverse. Licensed under CC BY 2.0.

8. Eco-ontology

(page 143)   McLevn, "Taxidermy Display of Winged Creatures." Openverse. Licensed under CC BY-SA 2.0.

(page 144)   mrdannynavarro, "Bird Eggs Light Box." Openverse. Licensed under CC BY-SA 2.0.

9. Re-commencement

(page 159)   LifeSuperCharger, "Dandelion Wish (88/365)." Openverse. Licensed under CC BY 2.0.

Index